Dr Peter Rawcliffe graduated from Pembroke College, Cambridge, and carried out his clinical studies at the London Hospital in Whitechapel. He subsequently worked in the Gastroenterology Unit at the Hammersmith Hospital, London and in 1979 moved to the Radcliffe Infirmary, Oxford. Here he has been involved in research into coeliac disease, and in particular in trying to define more closely the damaging components of wheat gluten. He and Ruth Rolph set up the Oxford Coeliac Clinic. He is now a General Practitioner in Oxford. His main interests are fly-fishing and gardening.

Ruth Rolph gained an honours degree in nutrition from Queen Elizabeth College, London University, in 1975. Following State Registration, she became a dietitian in Oxford and has developed a special interest in diets for patients with gastrointestinal disorders. She too is a keen gardener and enjoys aerobics.

THE GLUTEN-FREE DIET BOOK

A guide to coeliac disease, dermatitis herpetiformis and gluten-free cookery

Dr Peter Rawcliffe, MA, MB, BChir, and Ruth Rolph, SRD

Foreword by
A. M. Dawson, MD, FRCP
Physician to HM the Queen
Physician to St Bartholomew's Hospital, London

POSITIVE HEALTH GUIDE

This book is dedicated to Maggie Stopard

© Peter M. Rawcliffe and Ruth Rolph, 1985

First published in the United Kingdom in 1985 by
Martin Dunitz Limited, London

Published in 1990 by
Macdonald Optima.

This edition published by Optima in 1992
Reprinted 1994

British Library Cataloguing in Publication Data
Rawcliffe, Peter
 Gluten-free diet.
 1. Man. Intestines. Coeliac disease   2. Food: Gluten free
 dishes — Recipes
 I. Title   II. Rolph, Ruth   III. Series
 616.34
 ISBN 0-356-19675-5

Little, Brown and
Company (UK) Limited
Brettenham House
Lancaster Place
London WC2E 7EN

Phototypeset in Garamond by Input Typesetting Ltd, London
Printed and bound at Alden Press Limited,
Oxford and Northampton, Great Britain

Front cover *photograph shows: Strawberry sponge flan (left, see page 83); Pasta salad
(right, see page 43); Courgette and red pepper flan (centre, see page 65)*

CONTENTS

Acknowledgements   6
Foreword   7

Introduction   8
  What is coeliac disease?   8
  What is gluten?   10
  Dermatitis herpetiformis   19
  Living with the gluten-free diet   21
  Research   24

The diet   25
  What can I eat and what must I avoid?   27
  Preparing food at home   32
  Fibre and calories   34
  Eating out   36
  Holidays   36
  Children   37

The recipes   38
  Soups   39
  Salads and salad dressings   42
  Fish, meat and vegetarian dishes   45
  Breads and teabreads   68
  Puddings   78
  Pastries, biscuits and small cakes   93
  Cakes   111
  Sauces   120

Useful addresses   123
Index   124

ACKNOWLEDGEMENTS

We would like to thank Dr Sidney Truelove, Dr Derek Jewell, Dr Stephen Turner, Liz Todd, and Julia Giblett for their helpful comments on the manuscript. Mrs Joan Borin, home economist, tested many of the baking recipes. We also thank everyone else, including patients and local groups of the Coeliac Society, who contributed recipes, or helped in other ways.

We are grateful to Mr David Heath of Welfare Foods (Stockport) Ltd for supplying us with Rite-Diet gluten-free flour mix and bread mixes, and for generous financial support with the photography. And to Alison Dean, home economist at Welfare Foods (Stockport) Ltd, for her expert help and advice. GF Dietary Supplies Ltd and Carlo-Erba Ltd also provided gluten-free flour.

Mrs Zena Jennings typed the recipes to her usual high standard and with her usual good humour.

1985   *Peter Rawcliffe and Ruth Rolph*

The publishers are grateful to the following for their assistance in the preparation of this book: Peter Myers, who took the colour photographs, assisted by Neil Mersh; Mike Rose for art direction, Gina Carminati for styling, Lisa Collard and Alison Dean, who prepared the food. China lent by David Mellor Ltd and the General Trading Company, London.

The black and white photographs were kindly supplied by Dr David Ferguson (page 11 *right*), and Dr Chris Mason and Geoffrey Richardson (pages 10, 11 *left*, and 12), of the Department of Pathology, John Radcliffe Hospital, Oxford.

The diagram on page 9 is by David Gifford.

FOREWORD

Dr A. M. Dawson, FRCP *Physician to HM the Queen,*
Physician to St. Bartholomew's Hospital, London and King Edward
VII Hospital for Officers

Coeliac disease is a well-defined condition in which wheat gluten causes damage to the absorbing area of the gut so interfering with the nutrition of patients. It can cause a wide variety of symptoms, even though sometimes the gut manifestations are minimal. Keeping to a strict gluten-free diet can transform such patients' health which, in a number of cases, has been subtly impaired for many years before diagnosis.

But treatment does mean keeping to the diet. This book will help a patient enormously to understand why this is necessary and how to prevent such a regime from interfering with their life.

There is an excellent explanation of how food is digested and absorbed and the nature of gluten and how it damages the gut lining. The main body of the book gives valuable hints on how a diet need not interfere with an active social life both for adult patients and children. A great deal of advice is given about dietary requirements in general and, furthermore, how to make delicious food from gluten-free recipes, so helping patients to have a broad, varied and interesting diet.

All in all a good addition to the coeliac library: I advise every coeliac patient to read this admirable book.

INTRODUCTION

This book is for people who have coeliac disease – called celiac sprue or gluten-sensitive enteropathy (GSE) in North America – or dermatitis herpetiformis, and their families. Our aim is to help you understand your condition and to give practical advice on the gluten-free diet. The first part describes what coeliac disease and dermatitis herpetiformis are and explains the reasons for the treatment with a gluten-free diet. In the second part we give guidance on gluten-free cooking and over 120 tested recipes to help you enjoy an interesting and varied diet.

A word of caution
This is not a fad diet book, nor is it intended that it should be used for do-it-yourself diagnosis or treatment. Many of the symptoms of coeliac disease can also occur in other diseases. You should not, therefore, start a gluten-free diet unless it is prescribed and you are under medical supervision. There is no scientific evidence that this diet is of any help in conditions other than coeliac disease and dermatitis herpetiformis.

What is coeliac disease?

Gluten, a protein found in wheat and certain other cereals, is harmless to most people. However, in coeliac disease it damages the small intestine and so causes a variety of symptoms. We do not know why certain people are affected in this way.

First we shall describe the anatomy and working of the digestive system. When food has been broken down by chewing, and swallowed, it enters the stomach. Here it is further broken down, both mechanically and chemically. The resulting soup-like liquid then passes through the duodenum and into the small intestine (see diagram). The upper part of the small intestine is known as the jejunum. Further digestion goes on here and the food materials, which are by now well broken down, are absorbed through the intestinal wall into the bloodstream, and so distributed around the body. Anything that is not absorbed passes into the large intestine (colon) and is excreted in the faeces.

The small intestine, then, has an all-important role in absorbing the food you eat, so that it can be put to use around the body. When it fails to work properly, and food is no longer absorbed normally,

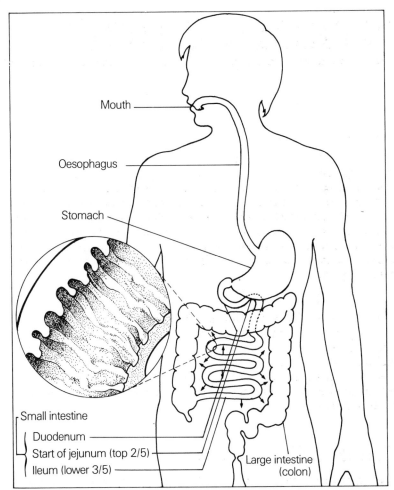

Mouth

Oesophagus

Stomach

Small intestine
Duodenum
Start of jejunum (top 2/5)
Ileum (lower 3/5)

Large intestine
(colon)

The digestive system; inset shows the circular folds of the small intestine, arrows indicate food being absorbed into the bloodstream.

this is known as malabsorption. Coeliac disease is an important (but not the only) cause of malabsorption. Malabsorption of food results in weight loss and deficiencies of vitamins and minerals.

The small intestine under the microscope

The small intestine is a tube about 6.5 metres (20 ft) long and 4 cm (1½ in) in diameter. Its most remarkable feature is that its lining, called the mucosa, over which the food passes, is very highly folded. First, the tube itself has a series of large circular folds in its surface. Next, looking at the mucosa under the microscope we can see numerous finger-like projections: these are known as villi. Each villus is between 0.2 and 1 mm long and can just be made out with the

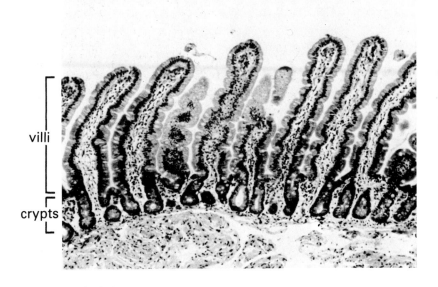

villi

crypts

A cross-section of the lining of the normal jejunum with its long, finger-shaped villi (x 130).

naked eye. A cross-section of a villus at a higher magnification shows a covering layer of tall cells (called enterocytes), and a central core containing, amongst other things, small blood vessels. Finally, if we look at the edge of a single villus at a very high magnification using an electron microscope we can see that on the surface of each enterocyte there is a regular array of minute projections (about 600 per cell): these are known as microvilli. Overall, because of all these foldings, one on another, the surface area of the small intestine is enormous. It has been estimated that the total area in an adult is about that of a tennis court!

During digestion the food particles are further broken down on the surface of the enterocytes before passing through the cells and reaching the blood vessels in the villi. From there they are transported away, in the blood, around the body.

In coeliac disease this process is upset because there is considerable damage to the mucosa, caused by gluten.

What is gluten?

Gluten is a protein (or, more accurately, a mixture of many very

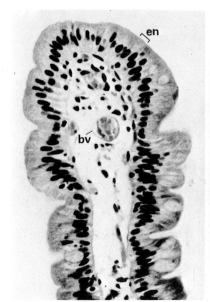 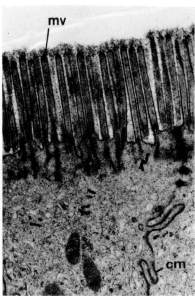

Left The tip of a villus in cross-section (x 350); note blood vessels (bv) within and the enterocytes (en) of the surface layer. *Right* Part of a single enterocyte, showing the surface microvilli (x 20,000); mv – microvillus, cm – outer cell membrane.

similar proteins) that is found in several grain crops. The main source in the Western diet is wheat. The bulk of the wheat seed or grain, which forms the food reserve for the new seedling, is milled to produce flour. Flour has two major components – starch and proteins; the main protein is gluten. This is a very sticky material – the word gluten is a Latin one meaning glue, hence the adjective glutinous – and it is largely responsible for the excellent breadmaking qualities of wheat flour, giving it the characteristic doughy feel when mixed with water.

Some other cereals have similar proteins which, like wheat gluten, are also damaging to your intestine if you have coeliac disease. Rye and barley are certainly damaging but there is still doubt about oats (see page 30). Rice and maize are not harmful.

What effect does gluten have on the intestine in coeliac disease?

In coeliac disease the mucosa of the intestine is badly damaged by gluten. You can see this very clearly in the photograph overleaf. The villi are almost completely lost, only a few small bumps remaining. This appearance is often called a 'flat' mucosa and the villi are described as atrophic. Any microvilli that remain are shortened and irregular. Not surprisingly, the result of this damage, with the loss

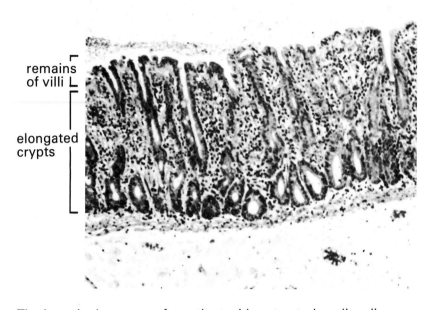

remains
of villi

elongated
crypts

The intestinal mucosa of a patient with untreated coeliac disease.
The surface is almost flat, with only the remnants of villi to be
seen (x 130).

of healthy enterocytes and reduction of surface area, results in malabsorption. Malabsorption can lead to weight loss and deficiencies of
vitamins and minerals. In the case shown in the photograph, the lady
came to us with severe anaemia due to a shortage of iron. Although
she had been taking iron tablets as well as her normal diet, she had
been absorbing so little that a deficiency had developed.

What are the symptoms of coeliac disease?   The damage to the
intestine can lead to many different symptoms. The commonest are:

Babies and children	**Adults**
Miserable baby, crying and irritable	Weight loss
	Diarrhoea
Failure to put on weight or gain height normally	Anaemia
	Tiredness and weakness
Diarrhoea	Abdominal discomfort and rumbling
	Recurrent mouth ulcers
	Sore tongue
	Bone pain (due to soft bones)

People vary greatly in the symptoms they have. Fortunately, not everyone has every symptom! Any pattern can occur: some people have one of the more unusual symptoms without having any of the commoner ones. None is characteristic of coeliac disease alone – similar symptoms can occur in other conditions. We describe later the tests that have to be carried out to narrow down the possibilities, and finally to decide whether or not someone has coeliac disease.

Who gets coeliac disease?

Both sexes are equally affected and both children and adults can develop the disease. Babies may begin to have symptoms as soon as they start on gluten-containing foods when they are weaned at about three to four months. The first appearance of symptoms is common from then on until ten to twelve years old. It is unusual for the condition to start during the teens. It most commonly begins between the ages of twenty and fifty. People can develop the disease even later – one of our patients in Oxford was eighty-six when she became unwell – though this is unusual. We do not know why some people are affected as children but others don't get symptoms until later in life.

How common is it?

Coeliac disease occurs in many parts of the world including Europe, North America and Australasia. It is very rarely diagnosed in India, Africa or China. There are probably several reasons for this. Dietary habits are different and people in these countries eat little gluten. Medical care is often less advanced than we are used to: people more readily accept ill-health and so the cause may remain undiagnosed. There may well be genetic reasons too, with some races being less likely to develop the condition. Probably it is a combination of these factors, and maybe others we are not aware of.

In the United Kingdom about 1 in 2000 to 3000 of the population are known to have coeliac disease, though there are certainly others who have not been diagnosed. Coeliac disease is particularly common in Ireland, especially on the west coast, where 1 in 200 to 300 people are affected. In Scandinavia the figure is about 1 in 4000. We don't have reliable figures for North America but the condition does not seem to be as common as it is in the UK. A figure of 1 in 5000 has been suggested.

An inherited condition?

We have known for a long time that coeliac disease tends to run in families. Certain chemicals, called the HLA antigens, are carried on everybody's white blood cells and are known to be inherited – like the chemicals on the red blood cells which give you a particular blood group. Recent research has shown that these HLA antigens are found in a particular combination much more often in people with coeliac disease than in the rest of the population, so it seems that a person's genetic make-up is important in the development of the disease.

However, there have been a number of cases where only one of a pair of identical twins has developed the condition. As they are by definition genetically identical, there must be other factors than hereditary ones. A difference in the amount of gluten eaten is one possibility, but in many of the twins studied the intake has been very similar, so it looks as if there are other unidentified factors.

Although the way coeliac disease is inherited is complicated and not completely understood, some answers can be given to three practical questions that are often asked:

You say that coeliac disease is inherited. If that is the case why is it that none of my relatives has it?   This is not uncommon. There are several possible reasons. Firstly, you may simply not know enough about your relatives' medical histories. Sometimes when people go into their family history more thoroughly they do come across someone else with the condition. Secondly, there are undoubtedly people with a mild form of the disease who may never develop symptoms bad enough to take them to the doctor. This must have applied even more in the past than it does today. Again, minor symptoms may be attributed to other causes by the doctor as well as by the patient. Thirdly, we do know from careful studies done on several generations of families with coeliac disease, that the condition can skip generations. Finally, the condition has been known by other names in the past, including idiopathic steatorrhoea and sprue.

What are the chances of my children having the condition?   If you or your partner have coeliac disease then there is approximately a one in ten chance that any one of your children will have the condition. As it is readily and effectively treated there is no reason for you to limit the size of your family on this account.

My child is perfectly well but is there any way you can tell whether he or she will develop coeliac disease later on?   The short answer is no. While the pattern of the HLA antigens (see page 13) gives some idea, it is not very precise. If your child has the 'coeliac' pattern of the antigens it makes it more likely, but not inevitable, that he or she will develop the condition. On the other hand, not having this pattern, though it makes it much less likely, does not guarantee that the condition will not develop. In the future this test may be improved but at the moment it is not very helpful on its own. We believe people should not worry as long as their children are well and growing normally. Many of the routine checks done at baby clinics are aimed at spotting anything going wrong at an early stage. If your child does develop any symptoms that cause you concern, discuss them with your family doctor, who will be able to arrange tests and ask for a specialist opinion if necessary.

How is coeliac disease diagnosed?

Anyone who has already been diagnosed may prefer to skip this section. For readers who are beginning tests or who have a child being investigated we hope to give some idea about what is being done and why, and what you may expect. Every case is different, and the tests needed to exclude other conditions vary considerably. The tests also vary from one hospital to another, and are not always done in the same order. For these reasons this can only be a rough guide. If you are in doubt about what is happening, do not be afraid to ask: most doctors are much more willing to spend time explaining things than you may imagine.

Many diseases can be diagnosed without any special tests. The rash of chickenpox, for example, can usually be recognized as soon as it appears. The diagnosis of coeliac disease is inevitably slower. It starts with your first visit to your family doctor to discuss your or your child's symptoms. Your doctor will enquire further into your story asking about other symptoms, about your family and so on, and will usually examine you at this stage. As we said earlier, the symptoms of coeliac disease can be due to many other causes, some of which will get better on their own. Particularly if your symptoms are not too severe, your doctor may decide to wait and see whether this happens. If your symptoms persist, if they are very troublesome or if there are special clues, such as a family history, the doctor will next ask for blood tests to be done. Depending on what they show, your doctor may want to do more tests to narrow down the possibilities further, or may decide to send you to a hospital specialist.

Which specialist you see will depend on your main symptoms. If, for example, you are severely anaemic, you may see a haematologist (blood specialist), while you are likely to go to a general physician or a gastroenterologist (specialist in intestinal disease) if your main symptom is diarrhoea. Children normally see a child specialist (paediatrician) whatever their symptoms. Most people are seen in an outpatient clinic – your doctor will arrange for you to go into hospital only if you are very unwell.

The clinic will have a letter from your family doctor giving the main points of your story, and the doctor will go over these with you. You will then be given a general physical examination. You will be weighed and asked to give a urine sample. The doctor will tell you what the most likely causes of your symptoms are and which tests still have to be done before a final diagnosis can be made so you probably won't need to go into hospital. The tests vary so much according to the circumstances that it is not possible, neither would it be very useful, to describe them all here. They will certainly include further blood tests. Ask about arrangements for the others – for example, how much time you will need to take off work, whether you will have to come into hospital, or whether you will be able to drive home after a particular test.

You will be given a further appointment to be told the results. If coeliac disease is still a possibility you will need to have a jejunal biopsy.

Jejunal biopsy

This involves swallowing a tube with a small metal capsule at its tip, to take a small sample (biopsy) of the intestinal lining, the jejunal mucosa. The test is not painful. The arrangements for carrying it out vary from place to place. You may go into hospital overnight (children usually do) or you may have the test done as an outpatient. Depending on the type of capsule used, and also because of variation between people, it can take anything from ten minutes to two to three hours to obtain satisfactory specimens. The test is usually done by a doctor but in some larger hospitals where many biopsies are carried out a specialist nurse does it.

You will not be put to sleep. The doctor may decide to give you a mild sedative beforehand though most people get on very well without one. In the case of young children a strong sedative is prescribed. The back of your throat may be sprayed with a local anaesthetic immediately before the test. If so, you should not eat or drink afterwards until the effects of the spray have completely worn off: the doctor carrying out the test will tell you about this but if you are unsure, ask.

During the test the position of the tube in your intestine will be checked by X-ray. For women of childbearing age it is usual to arrange the test at a time when they cannot be pregnant, even without knowing, as X-rays can be harmful to the baby. This means that the test is done during the ten days immediately following the start of a menstrual period. If you have any reason to think that you may be pregnant then of course you must let your doctor know. But if you are very certain that you could not be pregnant and there is some urgency to get on with the test, it may be decided to go ahead without waiting for a period. This is a matter for your doctor.

In some hospitals the biopsy is taken using a larger tube known as an endoscope. Because of its size you will be given an injection to put you almost to sleep and will have a hospital bed for the day, so that you are able to sleep off the sedation afterwards. X-rays are not used for this procedure (called an endoscopy).

For either capsule or endoscopic biopsy you may be asked to sign a consent form for yourself or your child.

After the capsule biopsy you will probably be allowed home straightaway, provided you have not had sedation, and in that case will be able to drive yourself if you want. If you have had sedation for either capsule or endoscopic biopsy you should not drive or work with potentially dangerous machinery for about twenty-four hours: the exact time will depend on the sedative used.

The biopsy will be looked at under a low power microscope and then sent for more detailed examination by a pathologist. If coeliac disease is confirmed you will now begin your treatment with a gluten-free diet. To clinch the diagnosis your doctor will want to do a further jejunal biopsy after you have been on the diet for three to six months – the exact time is not important. This is to make sure that the intestine has recovered satisfactorily.

When there is doubt about the diagnosis a gluten challenge may be necessary. This simply means going back to eating gluten again after the second, improved, biopsy and then having another biopsy. If you have coeliac disease it will show damage again. A gluten challenge is very often necessary in babies and children but less often in adults: you must be guided by your doctor on whether you or your child need one.

There is no standardized procedure for the challenge. Your doctor may ask you just to return to eating a normal diet; but he or she may ask you to eat a minimum amount of bread, say two to three slices each day, and sometimes to add gluten in powder form. Occasionally people get symptoms, especially of abdominal discomfort or diarrhoea, in the first few days of a gluten challenge. These almost always settle down within a week or so and the challenge can continue. Symptoms are less likely if you begin the challenge gradually, introducing a little more gluten each day over the course of a week, until you are back to a normal diet. As the challenge continues you may begin to develop symptoms again – for example, you may begin to feel tired, or your stools may become looser. The time it takes for this to happen varies.

To be sure of a clear-cut answer to the challenge, your doctor will arrange for a biopsy to be done some weeks after you start it, unless you get troublesome symptoms beforehand, in which case the biopsy will be brought forward.

How is coeliac disease treated?

In the second century AD, Aretaeus, a physician from Cappadocia (one of the eastern departments of the Roman Empire, today part of Turkey) who practised possibly in Rome, gave the first description of malabsorption. He also made some suggestions for treatment:

> In the first place, there is need of the juice of the plantain with water made astringent by myrtles or quinces. The stone of an unripe grape is also a very good thing . . . potions made with ginger and pepper and the fruit of the wild parsley which is found among the rocks.

Later authors gave similar descriptions, with even less palatable remedies. Robert Lovell of Oxford, England, writing in 1661, and quoting Pliny, says that 'the hee-goat spleen rosteth helpeth the coeliack'. It was not until 1888 that, in his paper *On the Coeliac Affection*, Samuel Gee of London gave the first clear description of coeliac disease as a specific condition. Gee ends his paper with the comment that 'if the patient can be cured at all, it must be by means of diet'. He would be pleased to know how right he has been proved.

It was not until after the Second World War that it became clear what the diet should be. Dr W. K. Dicke and his colleagues, working in the Netherlands, noticed that children with coeliac disease, who had been making good progress under conditions of near starvation during the German occupation, began to do less well when wheat and rye again became available. During the next few years it was found that it was the gluten in wheat and rye that was harmful.

In 1954 Dr John Paulley of Ipswich in England noticed the atrophy of the villi in the intestines of people with untreated coeliac disease (see page 11). A few years later it was discovered that the villi grew again when gluten was taken out of the diet, and that damage came back if gluten was reintroduced.

The treatment for coeliac disease is therefore a strict gluten-free diet. Gluten damages the intestinal mucosa whenever you eat it, and if you continue to eat it, symptoms develop. Even small amounts taken regularly can be enough to cause real damage. The sensitivity continues indefinitely so you will need to remain on a gluten-free diet for the rest of your life.

How quickly will I feel better on the diet?

Once you start a gluten-free diet the intestine begins to recover. The mucosa regrows and works normally again so that food is properly absorbed. This does not happen overnight; it will take several weeks or months for complete recovery. Some people begin to feel better almost straightaway, but in many cases it is three to four weeks before a definite change is noticed. A few people do not notice much improvement until six to eight weeks after starting the diet and this is especially true if you have been very anaemic. You will remain well as long as you avoid gluten.

What happens if I lapse on my diet?

If you eat gluten the intestine will be damaged again and you will become unwell. In a study of adult and teenage patients from St Bartholomew's Hospital in London it was found that if they went back on to a normal diet severe damage to the mucosa developed in more than half within three weeks. In all the adults there was severe damage within seven weeks, though in some of the teenagers it took longer. There is of course mild damage much sooner. We know that gluten causes damage within a few hours of being eaten and repeated small amounts can add up to produce more severe damage. Symptoms are not a reliable guide to the state of the intestine as some people can have quite severe damage before they start to feel unwell. Therefore, while an occasional unintentional lapse is not a cause for alarm, you should not lapse unnecessarily. It is much safer to be strict so that your intestine is always working properly.

Other treatment

As we have already explained, coeliac disease can cause vitamin and mineral deficiencies. These include vitamin D, calcium, iron and folic acid. If you are found to have a marked deficiency when you are first diagnosed you will be prescribed an appropriate supplement, until your body stores are back to normal. By this time the diet will have had time to take effect and you will no longer need the supplement as you will now be absorbing enough from what you eat. Supplements are by no means always necessary, only when deficiencies are particularly severe.

When you are properly treated on a gluten-free diet, having coeliac disease will not in any way restrict you in your job, schooling, sport or other pastimes. The only difficulties that may arise are in managing the diet itself. The second part of this book gives practical advice on how to do this successfully.

Dermatitis herpetiformis

Dermatitis herpetiformis (called DH for short) is a very itchy rash that usually occurs on the elbows, shoulders, buttocks and knees, although it can appear anywhere including the face and scalp. It is not infectious. The spots are reddish and slightly raised and there are also small blisters that are easily broken by scratching.

DH is an uncommon condition which can affect both adults (most often between the ages of 20 and 50) and children, though the latter rarely. A recent survey from Edinburgh suggests that in that part of Scotland about 1 in 10,000 people has DH, but figures are not known for other areas. It affects twice as many men as women. If you have a rash that may be DH, your family doctor will probably send you to a skin specialist. Diagnosis will include taking a small skin sample (biopsy) for microscopic examination. The biopsy is taken in the hospital outpatient department. A local anaesthetic is given and the procedure takes only a few minutes.

What is its relationship to coeliac disease?
In 1966 it was found that many people with the DH rash had the same type of damage to the small intestine as is found in coeliac disease, although only about one-quarter to one-third of people with DH have intestinal symptoms, and these are usually mild. It is now known that about two-thirds to three-quarters of DH sufferers have a damaged small intestine, while in the rest it is normal. Though the damage can be as severe as it is in coeliac disease it is often less marked. As in coeliac disease the intestinal damage is caused by gluten and recovers when gluten is avoided.

There has been a great deal of controversy among doctors over how effective a gluten-free diet is in helping the DH rash, but most now agree that the rash does improve on the diet though it does not always clear up completely. If gluten is eaten again the rash tends to come back, though in a few cases this may not be for many months or even years.

We do not fully understand the connection between what happens in the intestine and the rash. Like coeliac disease, DH tends to run in families and both may occur in the same family. We know too that the HLA antigens on the white blood cells occur in the same pattern as in coeliac disease (see page 13), all of which suggests a similar genetic make-up in people with these two conditions.

Treatment: diet or dapsone?

DH can be treated with a drug called dapsone. These pills are very effective and the itchy rash disappears, or at least is greatly reduced, often within a few hours and certainly within two or three days. You will probably be started on dapsone as soon as the diagnosis is confirmed. The next step is usually to carry out a jejunal biopsy (see page 16), particularly if you have any intestinal symptoms similar to those of coeliac disease, for example diarrhoea or weight loss. If the biopsy shows damage, your doctor is likely to recommend a gluten-free diet. If there is no damage, treatment with dapsone alone will probably be continued. You should use only as much dapsone as is necessary just to keep the rash and itching at bay, trying to reduce it from time to time. If you also start a gluten-free diet you will gradually be able to cut down on the dapsone. Even if you are not on the diet the rash tends to come and go to some extent over the months and years.

You may wonder why everyone cannot simply take dapsone rather than go on the diet. For some people dapsone alone is a completely satisfactory treatment. There are, though, some possible drawbacks.

- To control the rash dapsone needs to be taken indefinitely. It can have various side effects, including damage to the red blood cells which may lead to anaemia. This is especially likely when large doses are being taken, in which case periodic blood tests may be necessary.

- One person in three or four with DH has intestinal symptoms or evidence on blood tests that they have malabsorption. Dapsone does not improve these symptoms or the malabsorption because it has no effect on the damage to the intestine.

The gluten-free diet can be a very useful treatment in such cases. It may take six months or more for the diet to be really effective, but by this time the dapsone can usually be considerably reduced, if not stopped altogether. Even when there is no evidence of damage to the intestine, a gluten-free diet may be worth trying especially if dapsone is having any side effects.

There is one other drug that is sometimes used in DH – sulphapyridine. In general it is far less effective than dapsone but is sometimes used if dapsone is giving problems. Sulphapyridine can, though, also have side effects and a gluten-free diet is often a better answer in the long run.

You will have realized that the treatment of DH is not entirely straightforward. Every case has to be treated on its merits, and your specialist is the best person to advise you.

Living with the gluten-free diet

After you have been diagnosed as having coeliac disease or DH and have begun a gluten-free diet, your doctor will arrange to see you again in a few weeks' time. This is to check that all is going well and that your symptoms and blood tests are showing the expected improvement.

Once you are firmly established on the diet and all the necessary biopsies are completed, you should keep in contact with the hospital clinic. If you move away, ask to be put in touch with a specialist in your new area. An annual outpatient visit is often all that is necessary. A blood test will be done which will show up any deficiencies that may have arisen if you have lapsed, even unknowingly, on your diet. This visit also gives you a chance to raise any queries you may have with either the doctor or the dietitian. If you are worried about anything before your annual check is due you can always arrange an earlier visit.

Children

Children will be seen at the hospital regularly, especially in the early years. Babies should also be seen by the family doctor and health visitor, usually at a well baby or child clinic, where they will be weighed to make sure they are growing normally, as they should on the diet. The weights are recorded so the baby's progress can be followed, and the measurements are best done at the same place each time. Older children should have their height measured as well. There is no general rule about how often these checks are necessary; it will depend very much on how the child is getting on, and the checks will be less frequent as the child gets older, but your doctor will advise you. On page 36 you will find practical points about the gluten-free diet for babies and children.

Teenagers

If you are a teenager you may find that sticking to the diet isn't always easy, especially if you have just been diagnosed. If you have had coeliac disease since you were very young it will be easier, as you will have learned how to cope with the diet over the years. As you are becoming more independent and away from home more and more, you may find it awkward and dull to stick strictly to your diet. Sometimes you may feel unwell soon after eating gluten – in a way this makes things easier as you will be less tempted to cheat. If you do not immediately get symptoms you may find the temptation to cheat harder to resist. If, though, you are still growing (and most people go on growing until they are about eighteen) lapsing on your diet can cause sufficient damage to the intestine to slow down your growth. This is because you are not absorbing food properly and you may end up shorter than you otherwise would be.

In your late teens and early twenties you no longer run this risk as your growth will be complete. You may also find at this time that you can increasingly eat gluten without feeling unwell, although the intestine will still be damaged. If you do have occasional lapses during this time and do not get symptoms you are unlikely to run into any problems or endanger your future health. Nevertheless we are not advising you to ignore your diet, only if it is sometimes particularly difficult to stick to, you need not worry too much. See your doctor once a year so he or she can keep an eye on you.

Within the next few years you will probably lead a more settled life and will find it easier to return to a strict diet to keep you fit and healthy. If you want to have children this is especially important, as the chances of your having a child are reduced if you are not well treated on the diet – this applies to both men and women. And women who are well treated have healthier babies.

Fertility and pregnancy

Women who have had children after starting a gluten-free diet have shown increased fertility, easier pregnancies and healthier babies when compared with women having babies before being diagnosed.

Most women with coeliac disease, whether or not they are on a gluten-free diet, are able to have children. However, fertility is reduced in women not on a diet; and while miscarriage is not particularly common in women with coeliac disease as a whole, it is more common in those not on a gluten-free diet.

Antenatal care is available to all women to make sure that the pregnancy goes smoothly and to deal with any problems as they arise. You should let whoever is responsible for your antenatal care know that you have coeliac disease.

You will feel better if you are on a strict diet. Women who do not stick to their diet often have diarrhoea and abdominal pain during pregnancy.

Blood tests are carried out at intervals to make sure that you do not become anaemic. There is no special risk of this if you stick faithfully to your diet, but if you inadvertently lapse on it, absorption of iron and folic acid may be reduced and anaemia may result. So the blood tests are all the more important for you. To be on the safe side your doctor may prescribe iron and folic acid pills during your pregnancy. But you must still take care that your diet is gluten-free because the absorption of everything that you and the baby need depends on your intestine being healthy.

If you have to go into hospital for any reason, when you arrive let the ward sister or charge nurse know that you are on a gluten-free diet, so this can be arranged for you by the dietitian.

Coeliac disease does not give rise to any particular problems with the birth itself. Babies born to well-treated coeliac mothers are, on average, of normal weight and are as healthy as those born to non-coeliac mothers. Babies born to women with untreated coeliac disease on the other hand are, as you might expect, smaller than average.

The message is clear: stick to a strictly gluten-free diet and your coeliac disease should not affect your pregnancy. It is important that you eat a diet that is well-balanced as well as being gluten-free. Your dietitian and health visitor will be able to give you any further advice that you may need. Provided your coeliac disease is well treated there is no reason why you should not breast feed.

Fertility in men   Coeliac disease sometimes causes infertility in men, and this too will improve on treatment with a gluten-free diet.

Your dietitian
The dietitian is an important person to you. He or she will explain the diet to you and give you practical guidance, fitting the diet in with your normal eating habits. If you don't usually do the cooking at home, take with you whoever does when you go to see the dietitian.

Your contact with the dietitian does not finish after your first visit. He or she will be available to answer any questions you have in the future – do not hesitate to ask.

The Coeliac Society
We would advise you to join your national Coeliac Society. The Coeliac Society of the United Kingdom, founded in 1968, is run by and for people with coeliac disease and dermatitis herpetiformis. There are local groups throughout the country, which hold regular meetings. The services and publications of the Society are available only to members (see Useful Addresses, page 123).

The Society produces a useful booklet, *List of Gluten-Free Manufactured Products*, which gives the brand-name foods that do not contain gluten. The list is updated in another of the Society's publications, *The Crossed Grain*. This is produced twice a year and contains articles covering a wide range of practical and topical matters affecting people with coeliac disease and DH.

The Coeliac Society is associated with the Coeliac Trust, which funds research into coeliac disease.

Similar organizations in North America, Australia and throughout Europe provide the same services.

Life insurance
People with coeliac disease are usually dealt with fairly favourably by life insurance companies. The company will require as full a medical report as possible. They like to know how severe the disease has been and how long it has been well controlled on the diet. There may be a moderate increase in the normal premium in the early years, but this will be reduced as the disease comes under control. After four to five years of good health on the diet, the premiums will usually be the same as if you did not have coeliac disease. With this

as a guide as to what to expect, if you shop around you should not have any problems in getting good terms.

How do I explain coeliac disease to other people?

Perhaps it is unfortunate that the word disease is used. People with well-treated coeliac disease are as healthy as anyone else. If you do not like to use the word disease when telling other people about it, you can call it a condition. How do you explain what the condition is? Strictly speaking coeliac disease is not an allergy in the scientific sense (where the word has a rather precise and limited meaning) but it is a useful term, readily understood by other people. Sensitivity is an alternative.

Research

Research into coeliac disease has centred on two main questions. First, what is the difference between the intestine of a person who has coeliac disease and someone who does not? There has been a good deal of work to try to answer this question and we now know much more about the way the intestine functions, both in health and disease, yet the answer still eludes us. We do not know whether the difference lies in the enterocytes lining the intestine or in the immune defence cells (mainly white blood cells) between the enterocytes and deeper in the wall of the intestine.

The other main area of interest is wheat gluten. We are trying to identify more closely which particular part of this very complicated mixture of similar materials is responsible for the damage to the intestine. Although gluten has been known to be the cause of the problem for thirty years, we have still to discover the answer.

It has been suggested recently that a particular virus (called adenovirus 12) may play a part in causing coeliac disease. This is not yet proven – we have to wait for more evidence. If it turns out that a virus is involved, it will probably be only one of several factors. Put another way, many people may be infected with the virus at some time in their lives, but only some may get coeliac disease. The timing of the virus infection (perhaps only if it is as a baby?), or the person's genetic make-up, may affect whether or not they develop coeliac disease.

What can we expect from research in the years to come? How long will it take to solve these questions? It is impossible to answer with any certainty. We are sure that the problems can be solved but we expect it will be a slow process. In the end, the increased understanding of both coeliac disease and of wheat gluten may produce new treatments and perhaps the development of a 'non-toxic' wheat that retains the necessary characteristics for traditional bread-making. On the way we will learn a lot about the intestine: this will help our understanding of other intestinal diseases whose origins are even more obscure.

THE DIET

For someone just starting a gluten-free diet, the prospect may seem daunting. The aim of this chapter is to show that this need not be so, and that the practical difficulties can be easily overcome. Having someone with coeliac disease in the family need not disrupt the rest of the household. Many foods are naturally gluten-free and can be enjoyed by all. The recipes offer new and interesting ideas in gluten-free cooking and eating.

Gluten is a protein found in wheat, rye and barley (see page 10). Although most of us eat it every day, it is not essential to our well-being. There are many countries where gluten is not eaten and where cereals such as rice, maize and millet, which do not contain gluten, form the staple diet. A gluten-free diet can and should be a healthy diet.

A healthy diet

Our bodies require a variety of nutrients. Fat and carbohydrate are the main sources of energy, and protein is essential for growth and the repair of the tissues. A healthy diet is one that contains sufficient amounts of each of these. Vitamins and minerals, while only needed in relatively small amounts, are also vital to many of the body's processes.

Foods have been classified traditionally into three groups according to their major component – protein foods (meat, fish and eggs) carbohydrate foods (sugar, bread) and fats (lard, butter and cream). Although this grouping has been useful it is an oversimplification and can be misleading. Almost all foods are a mixture of protein, fat and carbohydrates and can be grouped to take account of this. The table on page 26 shows this grouping as applied to a gluten-free diet. If you eat foods from each group in the recommended daily amounts, you will achieve a healthy diet. Requirements vary, according to age, sex, build and activity. The table also shows the increased intake needed during pregnancy and in childhood and adolescence. There are other foodstuffs not shown that add variety and pleasure to eating. Examples are sugar, jams, confectionery, butter, cream, cakes and puddings. These foods are high in calories so you should eat them only in moderation. (See page 34 for suggestions on reducing calories.)

Food group	Portion	Recommended amounts
Dairy products		
Milk	1 glass	Children: 3–4 portions
Cheese	30g/1oz	Teenagers: 4 portions
Cottage cheese	2 tablespoons	Adults: 2 or more
Yoghurt	1 carton	portions
		Pregnant women: 4
		portions
Meat, fish, eggs, pulses		
Meat, fish, poultry, offal	60–85g/2–3oz	2 portions
Eggs	1	
Beans, peas, lentils	1 cup cooked	
Cereals		
Gluten-free bread	1 slice	5 or more portions
Crispbreads	2	
Gluten-free cereals	1 cup dry	
Gluten-free pasta	¼ cup cooked	
Oats (see page 30), rice	¼ cup cooked	
Vegetables and fruit		
Dark green or yellow vegetables (spinach, broccoli, spring greens, carrots)	1 cup	1 portion or more every other day
Oranges and grapefruit	1	1 portion
Fruit juice	1 cup	
Strawberries, blackcurrants, tomatoes, cabbage, Brussels sprouts	1 cup	
Other fruits and vegetables including potatoes	1 1 cup 1 medium sized	2 or more portions

Preschool children need foods from each group each day. Because the requirements change as the child grows we have not included figures. Be guided by common sense and your child's appetite. If in doubt consult your health visitor or dietitian.

What can I eat and what must I avoid?

The table below shows the very large number of foods that are naturally gluten-free and which you can eat without any problem. If you look through the table you will see that many of the things you eat at the moment are included: the gluten-free diet may not be as bad as you first imagined!

	Gluten-free foods	Gluten-containing foods
Milk	Milk – fresh, dried, skimmed Cream – fresh, soured Cheese	Yoghurt* Synthetic cream* Cheese spreads,* processed cheese*
Meat	All fresh meat, including bacon, ham, poultry	Any cooked with flour or breadcrumbs Sausage rolls, pies Sausages,* beefburgers* Meat paste,* pâté* Canned meat*
Fish	All fresh fish, shellfish Canned fish in oil or water	Any cooked in batter or breadcrumbs Canned fish in sauce* Fish fingers, fishcakes
Eggs	Eggs	
Pulses	Dried peas, beans, lentils	
Cereals	Rice, maize (sweetcorn), buckwheat, millet Sago, tapioca, gluten-free semolina Oats – porridge oats, oatmeal (see page 30) Gluten-free flour, cornflour, arrowroot, potato flour, soya flour, split pea flour, rice flour	Wheat, barley, rye Semolina Ordinary flour

*These foods may or may not contain gluten. Check the ingredients listed on the label and/or the Coeliac Society's *List of Gluten-Free Manufactured Products*.

	Gluten-free foods	Gluten-containing foods
	Soya and rice bran Gluten-free bread, gluten-free crispbreads, gluten-free cakes and biscuits Gluten-free pasta	Wheat bran, wheat germ All ordinary bread, crispbreads, cakes and biscuits Ordinary pasta – macaroni, spaghetti, noodles, ravioli
	Cornflakes and rice breakfast cereals, gluten-free muesli (see recipe, page 78)	All other breakfast cereals and muesli* Baby cereals* and infant foods* Communion wafers (see page 31)
Fruit and vegetables	All raw, canned, dried and frozen fruit All fresh, frozen and dried vegetables, including potatoes Canned vegetables in water or brine	Pie fillings,* proprietary baby and infant fruits* Vegetable dishes including flour Canned vegetables in sauce (eg, baked beans)* Instant potato* Potato crisps*
Soups	Homemade soups using gluten-free ingredients	Canned and packet soups*
Puddings	Homemade puddings using gluten-free ingredients Rice, sago, tapioca, gelatin, jelly	Semolina, proprietary sponge or pastry puddings Dessert mixes,* ice cream,* mousses,* pie fillings,* canned milk puddings,* infant desserts,* custard powder,* canned custard* Cake decorations* Cooking chocolate*

---

*These foods may or may not contain gluten. Check the ingredients listed on the label and/or the Coeliac Society's *List of Gluten-Free Manufactured Products*.

	Gluten-free foods	Gluten-containing foods
Fats	Butter, lard, margarine, cooking oil, olive oil, fresh suet	Packet suet*
Nuts	Nuts	Dry roasted peanuts* Peanut butter*
Seasonings and sauces	Salt, freshly ground pepper, herbs, pure spices, vinegar, homemade salad dressings and sauces using gluten-free ingredients	Curry powder,* mustard,* mixed spices and seasonings,* stock cubes,* gravy mixes and brownings,* savoury spreads,* sauces,* chutneys and pickles,* salad dressings*
Sugars, preserves and sweets	Jam, marmalade, honey, golden syrup, molasses, black treacle, sugar	Mincemeat,* lemon curd,* lemon cheese,* chocolate and sweets*
Raising agents	Yeast, cream of tartar, tartaric acid, bicarbonate of soda, gluten-free baking powder (proprietary or homemade, see recipe, page 71)	Baking powder*
Flavourings	All food flavourings and colourings	Beef essence,* chicken essence,* milk shake flavourings*
Beverages	Tea, coffee, fruit juice, squashes, fizzy drinks, Complan	Barley water, cocoa,* drinking chocolate,* proprietary milk drinks,* vending machine drinks (see page 36),* tomato juice*
Alcoholic drinks	All except beer	See page 31 for information on beer (including barley wine, stout and lager)

*These foods may or may not contain gluten. Check the ingredients listed on the label and/or the Coeliac Society's *List of Gluten-Free Manufactured Products*.

You must avoid all food containing gluten. Remember that it can come from wheat, rye and barley, and possibly oats. Wheat flour is the main ingredient of bread and pasta and is used in cakes, pastries and biscuits. It is easy to know that there is gluten in these. However, gluten is present in many recipes in smaller amounts and it is often used in processed and convenience foods without this being obvious (see below).

Oats

When you cannot eat wheat, rye and barley the question of whether oats are allowed becomes important. At present it is unclear whether oats should be included in the gluten-free diet. Most people are able to tolerate them, but a few cannot. We allow our patients to eat oats freely and only very rarely does anybody have any problems. Very occasionally someone has mild symptoms such as diarrhoea or a rumbling stomach which seem to be related to eating oats. When this does happen oats are obviously best avoided. Most people though remain entirely well and their jejunal biopsies show a good recovery. This approach is supported by research in Oxford which has shown, at least in those patients tested, that oats do not damage the intestine, even when eaten in large amounts. Some doctors however believe that all coeliacs should avoid oats, and you must be guided by your own doctor.

Processed and convenience foods

Many manufacturers use flour not only as a thickening agent but also as a cheap filling ingredient. Its use may be obvious, in fish fingers, pies and sausages, or more difficult to spot – in stock cubes, mixed spices, pickles, spreads, or ice cream (see the table on pages 27–9). It is essential to check the label on individual products and you should avoid any containing the following:

barley	malt
cereal binder	rusk
cereal filler	rye
cereal protein	vegetable protein*
edible starch	wheat flour
food starch	

*Textured vegetable protein (TVP) and hydrolyzed vegetable protein (HVP) do not contain gluten, but if 'vegetable protein' is listed, avoid it.

Remember, though, that manufacturers can change the ingredients of products, so check regularly.

Monosodium glutamate is a flavour enhancer used in many products. Although its name is similar it has nothing to do with gluten and you need not avoid it.

The Coeliac Society of the United Kingdom produces a list of gluten-free manufactured foods. Some manufactured products have the gluten-free symbol (an ear of wheat crossed through) printed on

The crossed grain –
the gluten-free symbol

the label. Unfortunately not all manufacturers use this symbol so if you do not see it this does not necessarily mean the product is unsuitable.

If you are unsure whether a product contains gluten then it is best to avoid it. If you want to know more about a particular food product consult your dietitian.

Alcoholic drinks
Cider, wine, sherry, whisky, gin, vodka, rum and other spirits, martini and other aperitifs, and liqueurs are all gluten-free. Although spirits are made from grains including barley, wheat and rye, all protein is removed during distillation.

Unfortunately we cannot be definite about beer or lager. These are made from barley, and increasingly wheat as well, and both these are harmful. The grain is broken down during fermentation but we do not know whether this is sufficient to prevent it being damaging to the coeliac intestine. Draught beer, stout and homemade beers may well contain gluten and are best avoided. It is safer to choose another drink, but if you do want to drink beer occasionally, have a bottled or canned beer or lager – it is more likely to be gluten-free, although this cannot be guaranteed. Some people are very sensitive to tiny amounts of gluten and if beer does seem to upset you, avoid it altogether.

Drugs
A few medicines contain gluten. A list of these is contained in the Coeliac Society's manufactured products list, and in their magazine *The Crossed Grain*. Your doctor will be able to prescribe a similar medicine not containing gluten.

Communion wafers
Communion wafers contain gluten. Discuss what to do with your parish priest. Gluten-free wafers are available – ask your dietitian about suppliers.

Preparing food at home

Baking and breadmaking

Where wheat flour is the major ingredient in a recipe straightforward substitution with gluten-free flour does not always work. The main examples of this are breads, pastry, biscuits and cakes. For these, special gluten-free flours have been developed and special recipes are required. For this reason there are many baking recipes in this book and all have been thoroughly tested. As with all cooking, experience is important and you may not achieve your best results at the first attempt. As well as the recipes, you will find hints and tips at the beginning of each recipe section to help you become a skilful gluten-free cook.

The special gluten-free flours now available are the result of a great deal of development by the manufacturers and have been much improved in recent years. Cakes and biscuits made with them are very good indeed. It is only fair to point out though that while it is now possible to bake good and palatable gluten-free bread it is still not like ordinary bread. This is not surprising, as it is precisely for its glutinous qualities that wheat flour is chosen for breadmaking, the gluten giving structure to the loaf. You cannot expect things to be quite the same without it.

Gluten-free flours are different from normal flour to bake with. They are lighter and 'squeakier', some more so than others. There is a variety available. Some already contain a raising agent (self-raising flours), others do not (plain flours). They do not specify on the packet whether they are plain or self-raising, so you will have to check the ingredient list to see if there is a raising agent (bicarbonate of soda, yeast, baking powder).

Many people enjoy making their own bread, but if you do not want to do this, ready-made gluten-free loaves are available, tinned or in a sealed plastic wrap. There are also bread mixes (white and brown) which provide a good, quickly made, gluten-free loaf. Some bakers are prepared to bake bread for you if you supply the gluten-free flour. Your dietitian may be able to tell you if there is a baker in your area who will do this. Make sure the baker understands that your gluten-free bread should not be contaminated with ordinary flour. If you have a freezer you may find it convenient to bake in bulk (or ask your baker to do so) and freeze what you do not immediately need.

Other flours Potato, chick pea, soya, split pea, maize, rice, arrow-root, sago and buckwheat flours are free from gluten. They are available from most health food shops.

Baking powder Commercial baking powders may contain gluten, so check, or make your own using the recipe on page 71.

Sauces

Flour is also used as a thickening agent, for example in soups, sauces, gravies and casseroles. Even these small amounts of gluten are enough to be damaging. Standard recipes can be easily adapted replacing the gluten-containing ingredient with a non-gluten alternative. For instance, in a stew, while the meat and vegetables are naturally gluten-free, the stock (if made from a stock cube), white pepper, and flour used to thicken the gravy, are all possible sources of gluten. Using a gluten-free stock cube or homemade stock, freshly ground black pepper and cornflour is all that is necessary to make this dish gluten-free. A selection of recipes modified in this way has been included in this book and we hope that they will be particularly helpful to the beginner.

Availability of special gluten-free products

Gluten-free products are available in most European countries, North America, Australia and New Zealand. In some countries, including the United Kingdom, some products are available on prescription. In the UK these include bread, bread mixes, crispbreads, flour, pastas and plain biscuits. Less basic items, such as Christmas cake and fancy biscuits, are also made but are not prescribable.

It is worth checking regularly what special products are available as new ones are added all the time. Your dietitian will be able to tell you.

Your dietitian will also be able to tell you which chemists carry a good selection of gluten-free products. They tend to be the large town-centre chemists, but smaller chemists' shops will usually be able to order products for you, especially if you go to them regularly. In the UK people with coeliac disease are not classed as 'chronically sick or disabled' and so are not exempt from prescription charges. But children under sixteen, old age pensioners, some people

---

Special gluten-free products available

Flour and flour mixes (plain and self-raising)
Bread mixes (brown and white)
Soya and rice bran
Baking powder
Bread – tinned or vacuum packed
Biscuits – plain, savoury, fancy, filled (custard creams, chocolate, muesli)
Crunch bars
Crispbreads
Muesli
Pasta – macaroni, spaghetti, noodles
Semolina
Rich fruit cake
Communion wafers

---

on low incomes and women during pregnancy are. It will save you both time and money to buy a 'season ticket' for your prescriptions – details can be obtained from the post office.

Fibre and calories

Fibre   Unless you take care your gluten-free diet may be low in fibre (roughage). This is because most of the common sources of fibre such as wholemeal bread, some breakfast cereals and wheat bran also contain gluten. Fibre forms bulk in your diet and helps regular bowel action, so lack of it may cause constipation. It is easy to increase your fibre intake from other foods by eating plenty of fruit and vegetables; the skins are high in fibre so eat them whenever possible. Pulses, lentils, brown rice and nuts are also good sources of fibre.

Wheat bran cannot be used to give added fibre because it may be contaminated with gluten, but soya bran is gluten-free. Try taking about 2 heaped tablespoonfuls (30g/1oz) per day divided between two or three meals. Introduce it gradually over the course of a few days. You will see that soya bran has been included in some of the recipes in this book. It can be used in many other dishes too, for example, sprinkled on gluten-free breakfast cereals or added to soups, stews and casseroles. It can also be added to gluten-free bread and incorporated into many baking recipes. It gives the finished product a speckled appearance but does not alter the flavour. With experience you will soon learn which recipes are most suitable for added bran. Rice bran is also available but is not very high in fibre (rice bran is 8–10 per cent fibre, soya bran 70 per cent fibre). Neither soya nor rice bran is available on prescription in the UK, but they can both be bought from chemists and health food shops.

Calories   Most people gain weight when they start their gluten-free diet because food is absorbed more efficiently. This is often no bad thing if they have lost weight as a result of their illness. Sometimes though people find that they put on more weight than they would like. It is unhealthy to be overweight: several diseases, for example, high blood pressure, coronary heart disease and some types of diabetes are commoner in people who are overweight. It is easier to avoid putting on too much weight than it is to lose it later. If you do become overweight you will need to reduce your calorie intake.

The quantity of calories you are able to eat and still manage to lose weight depends on your age, sex, height, occupation and how much exercise you take. Your dietitian will be able to give you advice on a target weight and what intake you should aim for. Here are a few tips to help you to lose weight:

1. Restrict foods that are high in calories, mainly sweet and fatty foods. Weight for weight, fats have twice as many calories as

carbohydrate or protein. Not only is fat high in calories but there is evidence that in excess it has other harmful effects, for example, in causing heart disease. A report in the UK by the National Advisory Committee on Nutrition Education has suggested that the amount of fat we eat should be reduced by a quarter. A few suggestions about reducing calories in your diet, and fat in particular, are listed here. You may also find a 'calorie counter' booklet useful.

- Trim excess fat off meat and avoid frying.
- Use skimmed milk rather than ordinary milk.
- Use cottage, Edam, Gouda or other low-fat cheeses.
- Use low-fat spreads on bread and toast rather than butter or margarine.
- Use a sugar-free sweetener in drinks, in stewed fruit (add after cooking) and on breakfast cereals.
- Choose low-calorie soft drinks.
- Drink less alcohol. Alcohol has almost as many calories as fat.
- Eat more fibre. Fibre fills you up without adding calories.

There is still some dispute over whether some fats are more harmful than others, so the simplest thing to do is to cut down on all fat. Polyunsaturated fats are probably better for you than saturated fats (but remember they are just as high in calories).

2. Don't skip meals. Try to eat three small meals daily so you will be less tempted to eat snacks.

3. Exercise is good for you and will help to burn off calories. But be sure to start gradually if you have not been exercising regularly for some time. Do not rush into vigorous exercise straightaway. If you have any doubts about how much you should do, consult your doctor. Brisk walking or swimming are good ways for most people to start.

4. Above all you will need motivation, willpower and perseverance. If you cannot manage to lose weight on your own then joining a slimming group might help you. Do not worry that you are on a gluten-free diet – the group will still be able to help, though you should let them know about it when you join.

Calorie and fibre values are given with each recipe. You will notice that a fairly large proportion of the recipes are baking or pudding recipes. We have included these because they are the most difficult to make with gluten-free ingredients – but they tend to be high in calories. So if you have a weight problem you must be careful how much of them you eat.

Eating out

Do not avoid eating out. If you are careful you should not have any great problems. If you are going to eat out and are not sure whether any gluten-free food will be available, have a snack before you go.

At friends' If you are eating at friends', it is wise to let them know in advance that you are on a gluten-free diet and explain what you can and cannot eat.

At work If the kitchen at work can provide you with gluten-free meals this is ideal. Otherwise you can either choose gluten-free foods from the ordinary menu or take your own packed lunch. Drinks from vending machines may contain gluten.

Restaurants and hotels You can enquire in advance about the menu if you wish: you will find many chefs are pleased to help. If you cannot do this, try to eat where there is a wide choice available because you will have to choose 'safe' foods from the menu. For starters, soups are best avoided unless they are clear; melon and grapefruit are suitable alternatives. For a main course, it is wise to choose plainly cooked meats or fish without sauces or gravy. Fish cooked in a batter is not suitable. Salads are usually safe but be careful about any dressing and remember that processed meats may contain gluten. Many puddings such as pastries, sponge puddings, gâteaux, ice cream, flans and cheesecakes contain gluten. Order instead fruit salad, rice pudding, sorbets, meringues or baked custards, or cheese – without the biscuits!

In hospital If you have to go into hospital, try to let the dietitian or ward sister know in advance that you are on a gluten-free diet. Smaller hospitals do not always have stocks of gluten-free foods so take bread and biscuits with you. Not all staff will know about the gluten-free diet: if you are offered something which you think may contain gluten, query it, in case a mistake has been made.

Holidays

If you are staying in a hotel you will have to make special arrangements beforehand. Some hotels will provide a gluten-free diet if asked. It is wise to take a supply of gluten-free bread with you anyway – canned and prepacked breads are excellent for this purpose. If you are flying, a special meal can usually be provided, but you must give the airline company plenty of warning – most require several days.

Children

Children with coeliac disease are otherwise perfectly normal and will remain healthy provided that they keep strictly to a gluten-free diet. With babies this is easy to ensure. Many baby foods are gluten-free and clearly marked with the crossed grain symbol. When the diagnosis of coeliac disease has been made and you have started your baby on a gluten-free diet he or she will become less miserable. The baby's appetite will improve as the diet begins to work. Give regular feeds, allowing as much as the baby seems to want on each occasion. Do not give snacks in between.

As your child gets older begin to teach him or her about the diet. As time goes by children are able to manage things more and more for themselves. Try to fit your child's diet in with the rest of the family as much as possible so he or she does not feel too different. Your dietitian or health visitor will be able to help if you have any problems.

School meals
You will have to make arrangements about meals at school. Discuss your child's needs with the form teacher. If special meals can be provided (in the case of a boarding school this is obviously essential) you should try and arrange a meeting between your dietitian and the school cook. In any case, schools are now offering a wider choice of food and if your child is old enough to know what to avoid, choosing a varied and safe menu should be quite easy.

If gluten-free food cannot be specially provided and either your child is not old enough to choose, or there is not enough choice available, you can prepare a packed lunch. You could include cheese, cold roast meat or hard-boiled egg with salad, gluten-free crackers, or sandwiches made with gluten-free bread, plus fresh fruit or gluten-free cake. In the winter add a flask of homemade gluten-free soup (freeze in one-portion amounts) or one of the gluten-free ready-made soups.

Parties
Do not discourage your child from going to parties. Talk to the people giving the party beforehand to let them know what foods your child can and cannot eat. If you are giving a party, then all the food can be made gluten-free.

School holidays, outings and courses
Give the organizers plenty of warning: tell them what is needed and send food lists. Give your child a supply of gluten-free bread and biscuits to take along.

THE RECIPES

Weights and measures
The teaspoon (tsp) measurement used throughout the book equals
5 ml and the tablespoon (tbsp) 15 ml; both are level. Australian users
should remember that as their tablespoon has been converted to
20 ml, and is therefore larger than the tablespoon measurement used
in recipes in this book, they should use 3 x 5 ml tsp where instructed
to use 1 tbsp.

Calories (Cals) have been rounded off to the nearest 10, as have
kilojoules (kJ). Fibre values have been rounded to the nearest gram.

Unless otherwise stated, all recipes are to serve four.

Keep to either the imperial or the metric measurements in a recipe.
Gluten-free flours are more difficult to use than ordinary flours.
Accurate measurements are very important: measure all ingredients
carefully, especially the amount of liquid. Because flours vary, you
may find that more or less liquid is needed than is stated in the recipe
– always add a little at a time until the correct consistency is obtained.
Liquids should always be measured at eye level. Use the type of
margarine or size of egg stated in the recipe. Treacle and syrup should
be measured with a warmed spoon. Oven temperatures are given as
a guide but ovens vary so adjust to suit your own. Use the stated
size and shape of baking tin. This is particularly important for gluten-
free baking as the flours don't have the same structural properties as
ordinary flours and may need extra support. Non-stick baking paper
is useful and is available from stationers and department stores. Rice
paper is usually gluten-free, but remember to check.

Which flour to use?
Where any flour will do we have simply put 'gluten-free flour'. Plain
or self-raising flour has been specified where necessary. If you use a
self-raising flour instead of plain omit the baking powder and vice
versa. Add 4 level teaspoonfuls of baking powder to 450g/1 lb plain
flour.

Not all plain gluten-free flours (or all self-raising gluten-free flours)
have exactly the same properties as one another. Most recipes were
tested with Rite-Diet flour. In a few recipes where it is likely that
only a particular brand-name flour will work well we have indicated
with an asterisk which flour has been used in testing.

Freezing
Almost all gluten-free baked products freeze well. As they tend to

go stale quickly it is best to freeze them soon after making. Baking the small amounts needed for one person is time-consuming and uneconomical. If you have a freezer you can bake more at a time and freeze what you do not immediately need. We have indicated in the recipes themselves the few that are not suitable for freezing.

SOUPS

Tinned and packet soups may contain gluten. Homemade soups are good and satisfying. For convenience make in bulk and freeze in suitable portion sizes. Use gluten-free stock cubes or a homemade stock using any standard stock recipe.

Green pea soup
Each serving: 220Cals/900kJ, 3 g fibre

1 medium onion, chopped
60g/2oz margarine
2 rashers bacon, finely
  chopped
550ml/1 pt gluten-free chicken or
  ham stock

225g/8oz fresh (shelled) or frozen
  peas
salt and freshly ground black
  pepper
chopped fresh parsley

In a saucepan, cook the onion gently in the margarine until it starts to soften and turn gold. Add the chopped bacon and fry for a few minutes more. Pour in the stock, add the peas and simmer gently until they are cooked. Liquidize or rub through a sieve and dilute to taste with more stock. Season to taste. Reheat, sprinkle with the chopped parsley and serve.
  This soup is particularly good made with smoked bacon. Dried peas can also be used: 115g/4oz dried peas, soaked overnight, and the cooking time increased to 1 hour.

Tomato soup

Each serving: 100Cals/420kJ, 3 g fibre

15g/½oz margarine
10ml/2 tsp olive oil
115g/4oz potatoes, peeled and diced
115g/4oz onions, peeled and diced
450g/1 lb ripe tomatoes, skinned and roughly chopped

1 tbsp chopped fresh parsley
¼ tsp chopped fresh thyme
¼ tsp salt
freshly ground black pepper
1 tsp sugar
340ml/12 fl oz gluten-free chicken stock

Heat the margarine and the oil in a large saucepan. Add the potatoes and onions and fry for about 5 minutes without browning. Stir in the tomatoes, herbs (reserving some parsley for garnishing), seasoning and sugar. Cook for a few more minutes. Pour in the chicken stock, bring to the boil, cover and simmer for 15–20 minutes until the vegetables are tender. Rub through a sieve and adjust the seasoning. Reheat and serve piping hot, garnished with parsley.

Cream of celery soup   See photograph, page 47

Each serving: 240Cals/1010kJ, 4 g fibre

30g/1oz margarine
350g/12oz celery stalks, chopped
115g/4oz potatoes, peeled and cut into chunks
2 medium leeks, sliced
550ml/1 pt gluten-free chicken stock
¼ tsp celery seed (optional)
140ml/5 fl oz single cream

285ml/½ pt milk
salt and freshly ground black pepper

Garnish:
a dash of cream
celery leaves or fresh parsley, chopped

In a large pan melt the margarine over a low heat and add the celery, potatoes and leeks. Stir well, cover and cook for about 15 minutes. Add the stock with the celery seeds and a pinch of salt. Bring to simmering point and cook very gently for 25 minutes or until the vegetables are tender.

Purée the soup by liquidizing or rubbing through a sieve, then return to the pan, stirring in the cream and the milk. Bring the soup back to the boil and season with salt and pepper.

Serve garnished with a swirl of cream and chopped parsley or celery leaves.

French onion soup

See photograph, page 47

Each serving: 490Cals/2060kJ, 2 g fibre

60g/2oz butter, plus a little extra
15ml/1 tbsp vegetable oil
450g/1 lb onions, thinly sliced
2 cloves garlic, crushed
½ tsp sugar
825ml/1½ pt gluten-free beef stock

285ml/½ pt white wine or cider
salt and freshly ground black pepper
4 large croûtons gluten-free bread
170g/6oz cheese, grated

Heat the 60g/2oz butter and the oil together in a large heavy-based saucepan. Add the onions, garlic and sugar and cook over a low heat for 30 minutes, stirring occasionally until the onions have turned an even, golden brown. Add the stock and wine or cider, bring to the boil, cover and simmer for 1 hour. Season to taste.

Spread the croûtons with butter and place one in each soup bowl. Ladle the soup on top and sprinkle with grated cheese. Place under a hot grill and when the cheese is golden brown serve immediately.

Bacon and lentil soup

Each serving: 290Cals/1220kJ, 5 g fibre

115g/4oz (dry weight) green or brown lentils
15ml/1 tbsp vegetable oil
4 rashers smoked bacon, finely chopped
2 carrots, chopped
1 large onion, chopped
2 celery stalks, sliced

225g/8oz tin tomatoes
1 clove garlic, crushed
1.1 l/2 pt gluten-free beef stock
115g/4oz cabbage, finely shredded
salt and freshly ground black pepper
chopped fresh parsley

Wash the lentils thoroughly in plenty of cold water, and drain.

Heat the oil in a large saucepan and fry the bacon gently. Stir in the carrots, onion and celery, and brown carefully. Add the lentils, tomatoes, garlic and stock. Bring to the boil, cover and simmer gently for 50 minutes. Add the cabbage, and simmer for a further 10 minutes. Season to taste and serve garnished with the chopped parsley.

Minestrone soup

See photograph, page 47

Each serving: 260Cals/1090kJ, 4 g fibre

30g/1oz margarine
15ml/1 tbsp olive oil
60g/2oz streaky bacon, chopped

1 medium onion, finely chopped
2 sticks celery, chopped
115g/4oz carrots, finely chopped

2 tomatoes, chopped
1 clove garlic, crushed
salt and freshly ground black
   pepper
1.1l/2 pt gluten-free stock
1 tsp dried basil (optional)

170g/6oz leeks, chopped
115g/4oz cabbage, shredded
1½ tbsp rice
10ml/2 tsp gluten-free tomato
   purée
grated Parmesan cheese

In a large heavy-based saucepan, melt the margarine and the oil. Add the bacon and cook for a minute before adding the onion, celery, carrots and tomatoes. Stir in the garlic and seasoning, cover and cook gently for 20 minutes. Pour in the stock, and add the basil, if using. Continue to simmer for about 1 hour. Add the leeks, cabbage and rice and cook for 30 minutes. Finally stir in the tomato purée and cook for another 10 minutes. Serve in warmed soup bowls, sprinkled with Parmesan cheese.

SALADS AND SALAD DRESSINGS

Salads are naturally gluten-free and are not fattening. But watch the dressings – not only are they usually high in calories because of the oil, but they may contain gluten. Recipes are given for making your own French dressing and mayonnaise at the end of this section.

Maggie's salad

See photograph, page 48

Each serving: 170Cals/710kJ, 2 g fibre

2 red eating apples, cored and
   sliced
6 sticks celery, sliced
60g/2oz walnuts, chopped

45ml/3 tbsp gluten-free French
   dressing or gluten-free
   mayonnaise (see pages 44–5)
1 clove garlic, crushed (optional)

Put the apples, celery and walnuts into a bowl. Add the French dressing or mayonnaise and toss to coat the apples and celery well.
   The garlic may be included in the dressing.

Salad Niçoise

Each serving: 280Cals/1180kJ, 2 g fibre

200g/7oz tin tuna fish
a few anchovy fillets (optional)
1 crisp lettuce
½ Spanish (mild) onion, thinly
sliced
8 black or green olives

1 green pepper, seeded and sliced
4 tomatoes, quartered
2 hard-boiled eggs, quartered
8 radishes, trimmed
90ml/6 tbsp gluten-free French
dressing (see page 44)

Drain the tuna fish and flake roughly. Cut the anchovy fillets, if using, into 2cm/1 in pieces. Tear the lettuce leaves and arrange in a bowl. Mix the tuna fish, onion, olives, green pepper and anchovy pieces and place on the lettuce. Arrange the quartered tomatoes, eggs and radishes on top. Pour the French dressing over.

Hot gluten-free garlic bread goes well with this salad.

Pasta salad   See photograph, page 48

Each serving: 230Cals/970kJ, 1 g fibre

115g/4oz gluten-free macaroni
200g/7oz tin tuna fish
½ large cucumber, diced
2 large tomatoes, chopped
3–4 spring onions, chopped

60ml/4 tbsp gluten-free salad
cream, or mayonnaise (see page
44)
lettuce

Cook the macaroni as directed on the packet. Drain, refresh with cold water and drain again. Flake the fish into a bowl, add the macaroni and the other ingredients, except the lettuce. Toss, and serve on a bed of lettuce.

Kidney bean, courgette and mushroom salad   See photograph, page 48

Each serving: 70Cals/290kJ, 5 g fibre

60g/2oz (dry weight) red kidney
beans, soaked overnight in plenty
of cold water
170g/6oz courgettes, sliced
60g/2oz mushrooms, sliced
2 tbsp chopped fresh mint
(optional)

15ml/1 tbsp gluten-free French
dressing (see page 44)
salt and freshly ground black
pepper

Drain the beans and discard the liquid. Cover the beans in fresh cold water, bring to the boil, and boil for 10 minutes. Reduce the heat and simmer for 1¼–1½ hours or until the beans are tender. Drain and leave to cool. Steam the courgettes until just tender and allow to cool. Combine the beans, courgettes, mushrooms and mint, if using, and toss in the French dressing. Season to taste.

Potato salad

Each serving: 330Cals/1390kJ, 3 g fibre

450g/1 lb waxy potatoes, boiled and sliced
1 quantity gluten-free French dressing or gluten-free mayonnaise (see below)

1 tbsp chopped fresh parsley
1 tbsp chopped fresh chives
4 spring onions, finely chopped
salt and freshly ground black pepper

Place the potatoes in a salad bowl, pour on the dressing and mix thoroughly. Add the fresh herbs and chopped spring onions. Taste to check the seasoning and keep the salad in a cool place until needed.

Cucumber raita

Each serving: 20Cals/80kJ, 0 g fibre

280ml/½ pt gluten-free natural yoghurt
½ large cucumber, thinly sliced
salt and freshly ground black pepper

small clove garlic, crushed (optional)
chopped fresh parsley to garnish

Combine all ingredients and garnish with parsley. Serve as a side-dish with curry (see pages 51, 63).

French dressing

Each 15ml tablespoon: 100Cals/420kJ, 0 g fibre

90ml/6 tbsp vegetable oil (olive oil is best)
30ml/2 tbsp wine vinegar
1 tsp gluten-free prepared mustard (optional)

1 tsp caster sugar (optional)
½ tsp salt
½ tsp freshly ground black pepper

Put all the ingredients in a bowl and whisk together using a fork. Alternatively, put in a screw-top jar and shake vigorously. Any chopped fresh herbs may be added. Store in the refrigerator.

Mayonnaise

Each 15ml tablespoon: 100Cals/420kJ, 0 g fibre

¼ tsp caster sugar
1 tsp salt

1 tsp gluten-free mustard powder
45ml/3 tbsp fresh lemon juice

2 egg yolks   *15ml/1 tbsp wine vinegar*
285ml/½ pt olive oil

Into a warm bowl put the sugar, salt, mustard and 15 ml/1 tablespoonful lemon juice. Add the egg yolks and, using a wooden spoon, beat thoroughly together. Drop by drop, add half the olive oil, beating well all the time. When the sauce is the consistency of whipped cream add another 15ml/1 tablespoonful lemon juice. You can now speed up the addition of the rest of the olive oil to a thin, steady stream – still beating continuously. Stir in the remaining lemon juice and wine vinegar, and lastly mix in 15ml/1 tablespoonful boiling water.

Keeps well in a screw-top jar in the refrigerator.

FISH, MEAT AND VEGETARIAN DISHES

Pure spices, fresh herbs and freshly ground pepper, invaluable additions to cooking, are gluten-free. But beware of ready-ground pepper, which can contain gluten. Take care with stock cubes and mixed spices such as garam masala and curry powder as they too may contain gluten. The quantities given in these recipes are usually for fresh herbs, but if you are using dried herbs, use about one-third of the amount stated.

Beans and lentils are included in several recipes. Because all beans and pulses are gluten-free and high in fibre they form a very useful and tasty part of the diet. They are high in protein and much cheaper than meat or fish, and since they contain negligible fat they are lower in calories. Dried beans, after their overnight soaking, must be boiled rapidly for 10 minutes before simmering until soft.

Rice is gluten-free. Brown rice has more flavour than white rice and more fibre, vitamins and minerals. When cooking any type of rice always follow the instructions on the packet. As a general rule use 1 cup rice to 2 cups water with a level teaspoon of salt. But some brown rice may need more water and takes longer to cook.

Vegetables are also useful sources of fibre yet low in calories. They contain lots of vitamins and minerals. Do not overcook as this destroys a lot of the goodness. Potatoes are not as fattening as many people think, though adding butter to them when mashing, or cooking them by frying will greatly increase the calories. The skins are high in fibre, so scrub or scrape them rather than peeling and boil or bake them in their jackets.

Although meat and fish are naturally gluten-free, when they are cooked in casseroles or served with sauces or with gravy, you must take care not to introduce gluten – for example, thicken them with cornflour or gluten-free flour, as in these recipes, rather than with ordinary flour.

Meat is a good but expensive source of protein. However, even lean meat contains quite a lot of fat and so is high in calories. To reduce the fat trim off any visible fat and grill or braise rather than fry. Fish is less fatty, but again avoid frying – grill, steam, bake or boil.

FISH

Fisherman's pie

Each serving: 400Cals/1680kJ, 2 g fibre

450g/1 lb fresh cod or coley, skinned
salt and freshly ground black pepper
1 bay leaf
450g/1 lb old potatoes, peeled
45g/1½oz margarine
140ml/5fl oz plus 30ml/2 tbsp milk
30g/1oz gluten-free flour
2 hard-boiled eggs, chopped
grated rind 1 lemon
15ml/1 tbsp lemon juice
¼ tsp cayenne pepper
1 tbsp chopped chives
1 tbsp chopped fresh parsley
30g/1oz Edam cheese, grated

Heat the oven to 190°C/375°F/gas 5.

Poach the fish in water, seasoned with salt, black pepper and the bay leaf, for 10–15 minutes. Drain and reserve 140ml/5 fl oz of the cooking liquid. Boil the potatoes and mash them with 15g/½oz margarine and 30ml/2 tbsp milk. Melt the remaining margarine in a saucepan, add the flour and cook for a few more minutes, stirring. Gradually stir in the remaining milk and the reserved fish stock. Bring to the boil, stirring continuously, to make a fairly thick white sauce. Flake the fish and add it to the sauce with the chopped eggs, lemon rind and juice, cayenne pepper, chives and parsley. Season to taste. Turn into a 1 1/2 pt pie dish. Sprinkle with the grated cheese. Spoon or pipe the mashed potato over the fish mixture and bake for 20–30 minutes.

Cream of celery soup (*top*, see page 40); Minestrone soup (*left*, see page 41); French onion soup (*right*, see page 41)

Recipe suggestion

Mushroom and spinach penne.
Cooking time: 20 minutes.
Method: Hob.
Ingredients:
400g penne; 350g mushrooms, sliced; 300g spinach, washed; 150g mascarpone cheese; 100ml red wine; 1 shallot, finely chopped; 1 garlic clove, crushed; 1 x 15ml (1 tbsp) olive oil; a pinch of salt and black pepper; a pinch of rosemary.

Method:
1. Boil a pan of salted water and cook the pasta according to the pasta instructions. Meanwhile heat the oil in a pan and fry the garlic and shallot until soft.
2. Add the mushrooms and fry over a high heat until they just give up their juices. Add the wine and rosemary and cook until the wine has reduced (about 5 minutes).
3. Add half the mascarpone and stir until melted. Add the spinach and turn it over in the juices until wilted. Season with the salt and pepper. Just before serving swirl the remaining mascarpone into the pan.
4. Drain the pasta and serve with the sauce.

Our promise

We are happy to refund or replace any Tesco product which falls below the high standard you expect. Just ask any member of staff. This does not affect your statutory rights.
We are here to help:
Tesco Stores Ltd., Cheshunt EN8 9SL, U.K.
Freephone 0800 50 55 55, Mon–Sat, 9am–6pm.
Shop on-line at www.tesco.com

Storage

• Keep refrigerated.
• Use by: see front of pack.

Additional information

• **Bag:** plastic, recyclable where facilities exist.

300g ℮

Packed in the U.K. for Tesco Stores Ltd.
© Tesco 2006

Recipe suggestion

Mushroom and spinach penne.
Cooking time: 20 minutes.
Method: Hob.
Ingredients:
400g penne; 350g mushrooms, sliced; 300g spinach, washed; 150g mascarpone cheese; 100ml red wine; 1 shallot, finely chopped; 1 garlic clove, crushed; 1 x 15ml (1 tbsp) olive oil; a pinch of salt and black pepper; a pinch of rosemary.
Method:

1. Boil a pan of salted water and cook the pasta according to the pasta instructions. Meanwhile heat the oil in a pan and fry the garlic and shallot until soft.

2. Add the mushrooms and fry over a high heat until they just give up their juices. Add the wine and rosemary and cook until the wine has reduced (about 5 minutes).

3. Add half the mascarpone and stir until melted. Add the spinach and turn it over in the juices until wilted. Season with the salt and pepper. Just before serving swirl the remaining mascarpone into the pan.

4. Drain the pasta and serve with the sauce.

Our promise

We are happy to refund or replace any Tesco product which falls below the high standard you expect. Just ask any member of staff. This does not affect your statutory rights.
We are here to help:
Tesco Stores Ltd., Cheshunt EN8 9SL, U.K.
Freephone 0800 50 55 55, Mon–Sat, 9am–6pm.
Shop on-line at www.tesco.com

Storage

- **Use by:** see front of pack.
- **Keep refrigerated.**

Additional information

- **Bag:** plastic, recyclable where facilities exist.

300g ℮

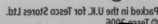

Packed in the U.K. for Tesco Stores Ltd.
© Tesco 2006.

Herrings in oatmeal

Each serving: 520Cals/2180kJ, 2 g fibre

4 herrings
salt and freshly ground black
  pepper

60g/2oz fine or medium oatmeal
60g/2oz margarine
lemon wedges

Ask the fishmonger to clean the fish and fillet them by splitting them down the back. Season to taste with salt and pepper. Coat both sides with oatmeal. Fry in the margarine until cooked through and lightly browned.
Serve garnished with the lemon wedges.

Baked stuffed mackerel   See photograph, page 59

Each serving: 330Cals/1390kJ, 6 g fibre

4 mackerel
salt and freshly ground black
  pepper
1 medium cooking apple
1 medium onion, finely chopped

60g/2oz gluten-free breadcrumbs
30g/1oz soya bran
2 tsp sugar
30g/1oz margarine, melted

Heat the oven to 180°C/350°F/gas 4. Grease an ovenproof dish.
  Clean and bone the mackerel (the fishmonger will do this if you ask him). Sprinkle with salt and pepper and set aside. Core and grate the apple, mix with the onion, two-thirds of the breadcrumbs, and the bran, sugar, salt and pepper. Place some stuffing in each fish and fold over. Place in the dish, sprinkle with the rest of the breadcrumbs and pour over the melted margarine. Bake uncovered for 20–25 minutes or until the fish is tender.

Smoked mackerel pâté   See photograph, page 58

Serves 8

Each serving: 150Cals/630kJ, 0 g fibre

2 medium smoked mackerel
140 ml/5 fl oz soured cream
115g/4oz cottage cheese
juice ½ lemon
salt and freshly ground black
  pepper

pinch freshly grated nutmeg

Garnish:
lemon wedges
watercress
pinch cayenne pepper

Maggie's salad (*top*, see page 42); Kidney bean, courgette and mushroom salad (*centre*, see page 43); Pasta salad (*bottom*, see page 43)

Skin the mackerel and remove the bones. Flake the fish and put in a bowl. Add the soured cream, cottage cheese and lemon juice and beat with a wooden spoon until smooth; or place all ingredients in a blender and blend until completely smooth. Season, add the nutmeg and a little more lemon juice if necessary. Chill for several hours.

Sprinkle a touch of cayenne pepper on top and serve garnished with lemon wedges and watercress accompanied by hot gluten-free toast.

Fishcakes

See photograph, page 58

Makes 12

Each fishcake: 150Cals/630kJ, 0 g fibre

*450g/1 lb potatoes, boiled and
  mashed*
*450g/1 lb cod or coley, poached,
  skinned and well drained*
3 tbsp chopped fresh parsley
*5ml/1 tsp gluten-free anchovy
  essence*
1 egg, beaten
10ml/2 tsp lemon juice
a little freshly grated nutmeg

good pinch cayenne pepper
*salt and freshly ground black
  pepper*

For coating:
2 eggs, beaten
*170g/6oz dry gluten-free white
  breadcrumbs*
45–60ml/3–4 tbsp vegetable oil
knob of margarine

Mix together the first ingredients in a large bowl. Adjust seasoning. Refrigerate for an hour or so, until the mixture is firm. Turn on to a board dusted with gluten-free flour and lightly work into a roll about 5cm/2 in diameter. Cut the roll into 12 slices. Dip each into the beaten eggs and coat with breadcrumbs. Heat the oil and margarine together in a frying pan and shallow fry the fishcakes until golden. Drain on kitchen paper and serve immediately.

Tartare sauce or parsley sauce go well with these fishcakes (see pages 120, 122).

Kedgeree

Each serving: 410Cals/1720kJ, 2 g fibre

675g/1½ lb smoked haddock
225g/8oz brown rice
85g/3oz margarine
1 onion, chopped
*¾ tsp hot gluten-free curry
  powder*

3 hard-boiled eggs, chopped
15ml/1 tbsp lemon juice
3 tbsp chopped fresh parsley
*salt and freshly ground black
  pepper*

Poach the fish in enough water to cover for 10 minutes or until cooked. Drain and reserve the liquid. Remove and discard the skin and bones. Flake the flesh and set aside.

Boil the rice in the reserved cooking liquid, adding water if necessary to make up the required quantity.

Melt 60g/2oz of the margarine in a large saucepan. Gently fry the onion until soft but not brown. Stir in the curry powder and fry, stirring, for 1 minute. Add the rice, flaked fish, hard-boiled eggs, lemon juice, parsley and remaining margarine. Season to taste. Warm through gently. Turn on to a warmed serving dish.

MEAT

Country pâté

Serves 12

Each serving: 150Cals/630kJ, 0 g fibre

115g/4oz streaky bacon, rind removed
675g/1½ lb lambs' or calves' liver
225g/8oz chicken livers
1 egg, beaten

30ml/2 tbsp double cream
10ml/2 tsp brandy
1 clove garlic, crushed
salt and freshly ground black pepper

Heat the oven to 170°C/325°F/gas 3.

Line a 1kg/2 lb loaf tin with the bacon rashers. Mince together the two kinds of liver and add the egg, cream, brandy and garlic. Season to taste. Mix well. Spoon the mixture into the loaf tin and smooth the top. Cover with foil. Place the tin in a dish with enough water to come halfway up the sides. Bake for about 2 hours. The pâté is cooked when it begins to come away from the sides of the tin. Leave to cool. Cover with a plate or greaseproof paper, put a weight on top and chill overnight. Just before serving, turn the pâté out of the tin.

Korma gosht (meat curry)

Each serving: 290Cals/1220kJ, 0 g fibre

30ml/1 fl oz vegetable oil
1 onion, sliced
2 bay leaves
1 stick cinnamon
8 peppercorns
8 cloves
4 cardamoms

450g/1 lb lamb or stewing steak
4 cloves garlic, crushed
15g/½ oz fresh root ginger, peeled and finely chopped or 1 tsp ground ginger
1 tsp chilli powder
½ tsp ground turmeric

1 tsp ground cumin	*salt*
1 tsp ground coriander	*chopped fresh coriander leaves or*
140ml/5 fl oz plain yoghurt	*parsley*

Heat the oil in a large pan and fry the onion until light brown. Add the bay leaves, cinnamon, peppercorns, cloves and cardamoms and continue frying for 30 seconds. Add the meat, stir in the garlic and the remaining spices and fry, stirring, for about 7 minutes. Stir in the yoghurt, add 285ml/½ pt of water, cover and cook over a gentle heat for 40 minutes. Add salt to taste. Garnish with coriander leaves or parsley. Serve with plain boiled rice and cucumber raita (see page 44).

Beef casserole

Each serving: 410Cals/1720kJ, 5 g fibre

30ml/2 tbsp olive oil	*2 sprigs fresh thyme or ½ tsp dried*
450g/1 lb chuck steak, cut into	*thyme*
cubes	*1 bay leaf*
225g/8oz onion, sliced	*salt and freshly ground black*
1 heaped tbsp gluten-free flour	*pepper*
15g/½oz soya bran	*115g/4oz field mushrooms, sliced*
285ml/½ pt red wine or dry cider	*115g/4oz smoked bacon, cut into*
1 clove garlic, chopped	*cubes*

Heat the oven to 140°C/275°F/gas 1.

Heat half the olive oil in a large heavy-based casserole. Add the cubes of beef and fry to seal on all sides. Remove them as they brown and set aside on a plate. Brown the onion in the casserole. Return the meat, stir in the flour and bran and pour in the wine or cider, stirring well. Add the garlic, herbs and seasoning and bring to the boil. Cover the casserole, place in the oven and cook for 2 hours. Fry the mushrooms and bacon in the rest of the oil and add to the casserole. Cook for a further hour.

Meat fondue

A meat fondue can be prepared in the usual way – see any standard recipe book. If bread is to be included as well you will of course use gluten-free bread. The following sauces are all gluten-free and suitable for both beef and lamb fondue: Sauce Tartare, Fresh Tomato, Barbecue, Spanish and Curry sauces (see pages 121–2).

Steak and kidney pudding

Serves 8

Each serving: 430Cals/1810kJ, 4 g fibre

Crust:
225g/8oz gluten-free flour
½ tsp salt
115g/4oz gluten-free shredded suet

Filling:
225g/8oz kidney

675g/1½lb stewing steak,
    trimmed and cubed
2 tbsp seasoned gluten-free flour
1 medium onion, chopped
8 large mushrooms, trimmed
30g/1oz soya bran
dash Worcestershire sauce

First make the crust. Mix the flour, salt and suet together and slowly add sufficient water to make a soft dough. Roll out on a board dusted with gluten-free flour and line a 1l/2pt pudding basin, keeping back enough to make a lid.

To make the filling, toss the meat in the seasoned flour and put it with the onion, mushrooms and bran into the prepared pudding basin. Add the Worcestershire sauce and enough water to three-quarters fill the basin. Moisten the edges of the crust, put on the lid and seal well. Cover with buttered foil, pleated to allow the pudding to rise, and tie around the neck of the basin with string. Stand the basin on an inverted saucer in a large saucepan. Pour in enough water to reach halfway up the basin. Bring to the boil, cover the pan and simmer for at least 4 hours, topping up the water as necessary.

To serve, remove the basin from the saucepan, take off the foil and wrap in a clean cloth. Serve from the basin with a spoon.

Liver and bacon hotpot

Each serving: 450Cals/1890kJ, 4 g fibre

450g/1 lb liver, sliced 0.5cm/¼ in
    thick
2 tbsp gluten-free flour
115g/4oz streaky bacon, rind
    removed and chopped
1 medium carrot, roughly chopped
1 stick celery, roughly chopped
60g/2oz swede, roughly chopped
2–3 large onions, sliced

1 tsp dried sage
salt and freshly ground black
    pepper
gluten-free stock or water
5ml/1 tsp Worcestershire sauce
900g/2 lb potatoes, peeled and
    sliced
30g/1oz butter, melted

Heat the oven to 170°C/325°F/gas 3.

Coat the liver slices in the flour and place in a shallow casserole. Sprinkle in the remaining flour. Add the bacon and prepared vegetables (except the potatoes) together with the sage and season with salt and pepper. Pour in enough stock or water just to cover. Add the Worcestershire sauce. Cover with a thick layer of potatoes, overlapping the slices. Cover the casserole and bake for 2 hours. Remove the lid and cook for a further 30 minutes. Brush the potatoes with the butter and brown under a hot grill.

Meat loaf

See photograph, page 57

Serves 6

Each serving: 290Cals/1220kJ, 1 g fibre

2 large slices gluten-free white or brown bread
45ml/3 tbsp milk
450g/1 lb lean minced beef
225g/8oz minced pork or gluten-free sausage meat
2 medium onions, very finely chopped
1 small green pepper, finely chopped

1 large clove garlic, crushed
15ml/1 tbsp tomato purée
salt and freshly ground black pepper
1 tsp mixed herbs
2 tbsp chopped fresh parsley
1 egg, beaten

Heat the oven to 190°C/375°F/gas 5.

Remove the bread crusts and soak the bread in the milk. Squeeze out excess milk. In a large bowl, mix the meats, onions, pepper, garlic and tomato purée thoroughly together and season with salt and pepper. Add the soaked bread, mixed herbs and parsley and mix again. Bind together with the beaten egg. Press the mixture into a 1kg/2 lb loaf tin and bake for 1¼ hours or until cooked. The meat loaf is cooked when it comes away from the sides of the tin. Allow to cool in the tin.

Serve cold, or hot with tomato sauce (see page 121).

Chilli con carne

Each serving: 460Cals/1930kJ, 23 g fibre

340g/12oz (dry weight) red kidney beans, soaked overnight in plenty of cold water
225g/8oz minced beef
15ml/1 tbsp vegetable oil
2 medium onions, chopped
4 tsp chilli powder
15ml/1 tbsp vinegar

1 tsp sugar
30ml/2 tbsp gluten-free tomato purée
140ml/5 fl oz gluten-free stock
400g/14 oz tin tomatoes
1 medium green pepper, seeded and chopped

Drain the beans and discard the liquid. In a large heavy saucepan, fry the mince in the oil, until browned. Add the onions and fry for a few minutes until soft. Stir in the drained beans. Blend the chilli powder, vinegar, sugar and tomato purée together and add. Pour in the stock and the tomatoes together with their juice. Season to taste and stir to mix well. Bring to the boil, partially cover and boil for 10 minutes, then reduce the heat and simmer gently for 1¼–1½ hours, stirring occasionally, until the beans are tender. Add the pepper 10 minutes before the end of cooking.

Pork in cider

Each serving: 450Cals/1850kJ, 4 g fibre

15ml/1tbsp vegetable oil
4 pork chops, trimmed
6 rashers bacon
salt and freshly ground black
  pepper
5 juniper berries, crushed
2 cloves garlic, crushed

1 large cooking apple, cored
  and sliced
2 medium onions, thinly sliced
140ml/5fl oz cider
675g/1½ lb potatoes, sliced
a little margarine

Heat the oven to 140°C/275°F/gas 1.
   Heat the oil in a frying pan and fry the pork to brown on both sides. Remove and place in a shallow casserole. Lightly fry the bacon rashers and, using a slotted spoon, put on top of the pork. Season to taste: do not oversalt. Spread the juniper berries and garlic on top of the bacon and cover with the apple and onion. Pour on the cider and finish with a layer of overlapping potatoes. Dot with margarine, cover with foil and a tightly fitting lid and bake for 3 hours. Place the dish, uncovered, under a preheated grill to brown the potatoes. Serve immediately.

Stuffed peppers

See photograph, page 57

Each serving: 280Cals/1180kJ, 5 g fibre

2 cloves garlic, finely chopped
2 medium onions, chopped
15ml/1 tbsp olive oil
340g/12oz cooked lamb or beef cut
  into small pieces
2 tbsp currants
salt and freshly ground black
  pepper

½ tsp ground cinnamon
½ tsp marjoram
400g/14oz tin tomatoes
4 red or green peppers
225g/8oz brown rice, cooked
20ml/4 tsp gluten-free tomato
  purée

Heat the oven to 190°C/375°F/gas 5.
   In a frying pan, fry the garlic and onions in the olive oil for a few minutes, then add the meat and the currants. Season, add the cinnamon, marjoram and two of the tomatoes and 15ml/1 tablespoonful of their juice. Leave, uncovered, to simmer very gently.

Meanwhile, cut off the stalk ends of the peppers and pull out the core and seeds. Rinse under cold water to remove all the seeds. Stand upright in a small casserole. Add the cooked rice to the meat mixture and mix thoroughly. Check seasoning. Fill the peppers with as much of the mixture as you can and put any remaining around the bases of the peppers. Top each with 5ml/1 teaspoonful tomato purée and pour the rest of the tinned tomatoes around the peppers. Cover the casserole and bake for 45–50 minutes or until the peppers are tender.

Lamb stew with dumplings

Each serving of stew: 450Cals/1930 kJ, 5 g fibre

8 dumplings, each: 130Cals/550kJ, 1 g fibre

*1 kg/2 lb lean stewing mutton or
  lamb
5 tbsp seasoned gluten-free flour
340g/12oz onions, sliced
225g/8oz carrots, sliced
2 medium leeks, sliced
2 large potatoes, sliced
salt and freshly ground black
  pepper
2 tbsp chopped fresh parsley or
  mixed herbs*

Dumplings:
*85g/3oz plain gluten-free flour
1 tsp gluten-free baking powder
¼ tsp salt
15g/½oz soya bran
30g/1oz hard margarine
2 tbsp chopped fresh parsley or
  mixed herbs*

Trim the meat, remove any excess fat and cut into cubes. Coat in seasoned flour. Put a layer of meat in a large saucepan followed by a layer of onion, carrot, leek and potato; season each layer with salt and pepper. Continue with the layers until everything is used. Add 1.1l/2 pt hot water, bring to the boil, skim off any surface scum, cover tightly and simmer gently for about 2 hours.

Fifteen minutes before the end of cooking time make the dumplings. Sift the gluten-free flour, baking powder and salt into a bowl. Mix in the bran. Rub in the fat, add the herbs and mix to a soft dough with 60–75ml/4–5 tablespoonfuls cold water. With floured hands divide the dough into eight balls.

Transfer the meat and vegetables to a heated serving dish and keep warm. Taste the liquid in the pan and adjust the seasoning. Bring to the boil and add more water or stock, if necessary. Drop in the dumplings, cover and simmer for about 15 minutes.

Arrange the dumplings around the meat and vegetables on the serving dish, pour over some of the liquid and serve immediately.

Meat loaf (*top*, see page 54); Lamb stew with dumplings (*centre*);
Stuffed peppers (*bottom*, see page 55)
OVERLEAF: Smoked mackerel pâté (*top left*, see page 49); Baked
stuffed mackerel (*centre right*, see page 49); Fishcakes (*left*, see
page 50)

Chicken with mushrooms and butter beans

Each serving: 330Cals/1390kJ, 10 g fibre

170g/6oz (dry weight) butter beans
30ml/2 tbsp vegetable oil
1 small onion, finely chopped
115g/4oz button mushrooms, sliced
½ small green pepper, sliced
½ small red pepper, sliced
225g/8oz cooked chicken

45ml/3 tbsp sherry
30ml/2 tbsp top of the milk
salt and freshly ground black
pepper
1 quantity white sauce (see page 120)
chopped fresh parsley

Soak the butter beans overnight in plenty of cold water. Drain, add fresh water to cover, bring to the boil, reduce the heat, cover and simmer for 2 hours or until tender. Add more water during the cooking if necessary.

Heat the oil in a large saucepan and gently fry the onion, mushrooms and peppers until soft but not brown. Cut the chicken into small pieces and add to the pan. Pour in the sherry and the top of the milk and season. Bring to the boil, partially cover and simmer for 3 minutes. Drain the cooked butter beans and add to the chicken mixture. Make the white sauce and stir it into the chicken mixture. Reheat and garnish with chopped parsley. Serve with plain boiled rice.

Jacket potatoes

Choose large even-sized old potatoes, scrub them and prick several times with a fork. Bake in a hot oven, 200°C/400°F/gas 6 for 1½ hours or longer. When cooked they should be soft when squeezed. Cut open lengthwise and serve with a knob of butter, salt and freshly ground black pepper or one or more of the following fillings (quantities for 4 potatoes):

Each potato, with filling:

115g/4oz Edam cheese, grated
200Cals/820kJ, 3 g fibre

200g/7oz bacon, chopped and grilled
350Cals/1470kJ, 3 g fibre

200g/7oz tin tuna, with 15ml/ 1 tbsp chopped fresh parsley
230Cals/970kJ, 3 g fibre

115g/4oz ham, diced, with 200g/7oz sweetcorn
210Cals/880kJ, 5 g fibre

Pancakes (*top, see* page 67); Pizza (*centre,* see page 66); Courgette and red pepper flan (*bottom,* see page 65)

VEGETARIAN DISHES

Butter bean casserole

Each serving: 290Cals/1220kJ, 13 g fibre

*225g/8oz (dry weight) butter
beans, soaked in plenty of cold
water overnight
400g/14 oz tin tomatoes
1 small onion, chopped*

*½ green pepper, chopped
salt and freshly ground black
pepper
60g/2oz Cheddar cheese, grated*

Heat the oven to 180°C/350°F/gas 4.
Drain the beans and put them into a casserole with the tomatoes,
onion and green pepper. Season to taste. Cover and cook for about
2 hours or until the beans are tender. Uncover the casserole, sprinkle
the cheese over the top, and cook for a further 15 minutes.

Mediterranean baked courgettes

Serves 8

Each serving: 130Cals/540kJ, 2 g fibre

*1 onion, chopped
45ml/3 tbsp olive oil
3 red or green peppers, seeded and
diced
2 cloves garlic, crushed
8 courgettes, trimmed*

*salt and freshly ground black
pepper
lemon juice
170g/6oz Edam cheese, grated
60g/2oz tin anchovy fillets*

Heat the oven to 200°C/400°F/gas 6. Butter a baking dish.
In a frying pan, fry the onion gently in the oil until soft but not
brown. Add the chopped peppers and garlic and cook for a further
10 minutes. Bring a large pan of salted water to the boil and cook
the courgettes for 8 minutes. Drain the courgettes, allow to cool, and
cut in half along their length. Using a teaspoon, scoop out a channel
about 1cm/½ in deep along each half courgette. Chop this flesh,
add to the pepper mixture and cook for a few more minutes. Put the
courgettes in the baking dish and season with salt and pepper and a
squeeze of lemon juice. Fill each courgette with the pepper mixture;
top with grated cheese and a strip of anchovy fillet. Bake for 30
minutes or until browned. Serve hot.

Lentil roast

Each serving: 460Cals/1930kJ, 9 g fibre

225g/8oz (dry weight) red or brown lentils, washed (soak brown lentils overnight)
1 large onion, chopped
60g/2oz margarine
3 tomatoes, chopped

60g/2oz cornflakes, crushed
115g/4oz Cheddar cheese, grated
salt and freshly ground black pepper
mixed herbs, chopped parsley or celery salt, to taste

Heat the oven to 180°C/350°F/gas 4. Grease a 1 1/2pt ovenproof dish.

Drain the lentils. Put them in a saucepan with 285ml/½ pt water and bring to the boil. Cover the pan, reduce the heat to low and simmer, stirring occasionally, until the lentils are soft and the water is absorbed. Add more water if necessary.

Meanwhile, in a frying pan, fry the onion in the margarine over low heat for about 10 minutes or until soft but not brown. Add the tomatoes and cook for 5 minutes. Mash the lentils, add the cornflakes (reserving a few for the top), the onion mixture and the remaining ingredients. Adjust seasoning. Turn into the pie dish. Sprinkle with the reserved cornflakes and a little more grated cheese if liked. Bake for 30 minutes.

Vegetable curry

Each serving: 150Cals/630kJ, 8 g fibre

15ml/1 tbsp vegetable oil
1 medium onion, sliced
½ tsp ground ginger
1½ tsp turmeric
¼–1 tsp chilli powder, according to how hot you like curry
½ tsp ground coriander
2 tsp salt
freshly ground black pepper
400g/14oz tin tomatoes
1 apple, cored, and sliced
handful mixed dried fruit (eg, currants and sultanas)
1 medium potato, scrubbed and sliced

a selection of vegetables, eg:
340g/12oz runner beans, stringed and sliced
2 medium carrots, scrubbed and sliced
170g/6oz cauliflower, separated into small florets
115g/4oz courgettes, sliced
115g/4oz marrow, seeds removed and cut into cubes

15ml/1 tbsp lemon juice
1½ tsp gluten-free garam masala

Heat the oil in a large saucepan. Gently fry the onions and ginger for about 10 minutes. Stir in the turmeric, chilli, coriander, salt and freshly ground black pepper. Add the tomatoes with their juice, the apple, dried fruit and remaining vegetables. Bring to the boil, cover and simmer until all the vegetables are tender. Stir in the lemon juice and garam masala. Continue to simmer with the lid off so that the sauce can thicken a little.

Serve with plain boiled rice and cucumber raita (see page 44).

Vegetarian pilaff

Each serving: 430Cals/1810kJ, 8 g fibre

15ml/1 tbsp vegetable oil
225g/8oz brown rice
4 sticks celery, sliced
3 medium onions, sliced
2 cloves garlic
½ tsp turmeric
60g/2oz dried fruit, eg, currants or sultanas
115g/4oz mushrooms, roughly chopped

115g/4oz red or green peppers, chopped
1½ tsp gluten-free yeast extract, eg, Marmite
15ml/1 tbsp lemon juice
freshly ground black pepper
115g/4oz salted peanuts
cress to garnish

Heat the oil in a saucepan and fry the rice gently until transparent. Add the celery, onions, garlic and turmeric. Stir and fry for a few more minutes. Add 550ml/1pt water, the dried fruit, mushrooms and peppers. Bring to the boil, stir, cover and simmer until the rice is tender and the water is absorbed. Stir in the yeast extract, lemon juice, freshly ground black pepper and nuts. Turn into a warmed serving dish and garnish with cress just before serving.

Savoury flan

A flan base can be made using either the shortcrust pastry recipe (see page 93) or the basic brown pastry recipe given here. Three fillings are given but other gluten-free fillings can be used.

Brown pastry flan base

Flan base: 870Cals/3650kJ, 9 g fibre

30g/1oz hard white vegetable fat
30g/1oz hard margarine or butter
115g/4oz Rite-Diet gluten-free brown bread mix

pinch salt
1 egg, grade 4 or 5

Heat the oven to 200°C/400°F/gas 6.

Rub the fats very carefully into the bread mix with the salt, taking care not to let it bind together. Beat the egg and work it in, bringing together to form a soft pastry. Add a few drops of water only if the mixture is too dry or crumbly. Turn on to a board well dusted with gluten-free flour. Roll out into a circle approximately 23cm/9 in across. Lift carefully on to an 18cm/7 in flan dish and press firmly against the sides. Fold in the overhanging pastry to form a double edge. Prick the base of the flan well. Line with foil and weight down with dried beans or rice. Bake for 10–15 minutes to set the pastry. Remove the foil and beans.

Flan fillings:

Courgettes and red pepper See photograph, page 60

Filling, for one flan: 730Cals/3066kJ, 1 g fibre

30g/1oz margarine
2 small courgettes, thinly sliced
1 small red pepper, thinly sliced
1 large clove garlic, crushed
salt and freshly ground black pepper

60g/2oz Edam cheese, grated
140ml/5 fl oz milk
1 egg, grade 2

Mushroom and cheese

Filling, for one flan: 590Cals/2480kJ, 3 g fibre

30g/1oz margarine
60–120g/2–4oz mushrooms, sliced
1 medium onion, thinly sliced
salt and freshly ground black pepper

60g/2oz Edam cheese, grated
140ml/5fl oz milk
1 egg, grade 2

Heat the oven to 200°C/400°F/gas 6.

In a frying pan, melt the margarine and fry the prepared vegetables for about 10 minutes. Season. Turn into the half-baked flan case and sprinkle with the cheese. Slightly warm the milk in the frying pan and pour on to the beaten egg. Adjust seasoning. Pour this custard over the vegetables, place the flan in the centre of the oven and bake for about 15 minutes or until browned and firm. Serve hot or cold.

Spaghetti cheese in tomato sauce

Each serving: 580Cals/2430kJ, 4 g fibre

115g/4oz gluten-free spaghetti
60g/2oz Cheddar cheese, grated
1 quantity fresh tomato sauce (see page 121)

2 tbsp gluten-free breadcrumbs
1 tsp dried mixed herbs
15g/½oz margarine
30g/1oz Parmesan cheese, grated

Heat the oven to 190°C/375°F/gas 5. Grease a deep pie dish.

Cook the pasta according to the manufacturer's instructions. Drain and rinse in cold water. Place half the pasta in the pie dish. Sprinkle with the Cheddar cheese. Cover with the rest of the pasta and pour the sauce over. Sprinkle with the breadcrumbs mixed with the herbs. Dot with the margarine and sprinkle the Parmesan cheese on top. Bake uncovered for about 30 minutes or until the top is crisp and golden.

Freeze before the baking stage. Thaw before baking.

Pizza

See photograph, page 60

Makes 6 slices

Each slice: 420Cals/1760kJ, 2 g fibre

1 recipe basic white scone mixture using 225g/8oz gluten-free flour and omitting the sugar (see page 73)

Topping:
1 medium onion, chopped
15ml/1 tbsp vegetable oil

3 fresh (or tinned) tomatoes, skinned and chopped
pinch sugar
salt and freshly ground black pepper
½ tsp oregano
115g/4oz cheese, grated
60g/2oz mushrooms, sliced

Heat the oven to 200°C/400°F/gas 6. Sauté the chopped onion in the oil for 7–10 minutes. Add the tomatoes and cook for 5 minutes more. Add the sugar, salt, pepper and oregano to taste. Set aside to cool.

Meanwhile, pat the scone mixture into an 18–20cm/7–8 in round. Place on a greased ovenproof plate or baking tray.

When the topping is cold spread on top of the base. Put the cheese on top and decorate with slices of mushroom. Put the pizza in the oven and bake for 20 minutes. Reduce the heat to 190°C/375°F/gas 5 and bake for a further 10–15 minutes. Freezes well.

For a change use a brown scone base (see page 73).

Yorkshire pudding

Makes 8 individual puddings

Each pudding: 100Cals/420kJ, 0 g fibre

*115g/4oz self-raising gluten-free
    flour**
pinch salt
1 egg

*285ml/¹/₂ pt milk and water (half
    and half)*
30g/1oz vegetable oil

Heat the oven to 220°C/425°F/gas 7.
   Place the flour and salt in a mixing bowl: make a well in the centre with a wooden spoon. Drop the egg and half the milk and water into it. Gradually work the flour into the egg and milk to form a smooth cream. Slowly add the rest of the milk and water and beat well. Heat the oil in 8–10 patty tins or in a 23×18cm/9×7 in tin, in the oven. When the oil begins to smoke, pour in the batter. Bake in the top of the oven until well-risen and brown (about 20 minutes for the small puddings or 45 minutes for the large pudding). Serve immediately.

*Tested with Juvela gluten-free mix

Pancakes

See photograph, page 60

Makes 4 small pancakes

Each pancake: 120Cals/500kJ, 0 g fibre

2 tbsp plain gluten-free flour
pinch salt
1 egg, grade 4

90ml/6 tbsp milk
20ml/4 tsp vegetable oil

Sift the flour and salt together into a bowl. Make a well in the centre, drop in the egg and 15ml/1 tablespoonful of the milk. Beat with a wooden spoon until smooth. Continue beating for 2–3 minutes. Beat in the rest of the milk. Leave to stand for at least 5 minutes. Alternatively, combine all the ingredients in a blender.
   Heat the oil in a 15cm/6 in heavy frying pan and when very hot pour it off into a cup. Remove the pan from the heat, stir the batter and pour in a quarter of it. Replace the pan on the heat and cook quickly. When the edge begins to curl, turn the pancake and cook the other side. Turn on to a hot plate and keep warm. Repeat with the rest of the batter, reheating the oil in the pan and tipping it out before cooking the next pancake.

Fillings
Sweet: squeeze lemon juice on to each pancake, sprinkle with 2 teaspoons sugar and roll up.
Savoury: fill each pancake with 2 tablespoonfuls of any hot savoury filling, eg, vegetables in a thick cheese sauce or minced leftover meat

or chicken in a mushroom sauce (see white sauce, page 120). Place the rolled-up pancakes in an ovenproof dish, cover with more sauce, sprinkle with grated cheese and reheat in the oven at 200°C/400°F/ gas 6 for 15 minutes.

BREADS AND TEABREADS

Gluten gives structure to bread and when gluten-free flour is used bread tends to be more crumbly and cake-like. There are a variety of flours and bread mixes available. It is best to use the type of flour stated in the recipe (self-raising or plain). The raising agents used are yeast or gluten-free baking powder. Yeast can be bought fresh from bakers or health food stores or dried from chemists, grocers and supermarkets. Fresh yeast will keep up to three days in a loosely tied polythene bag in a cool place, and up to a week in a refrigerator. It can be frozen but the maximum storage time will depend on the freshness of the yeast and the storage conditions before it is frozen. The yeast should be weighed out in 15g/½ oz or 30g/1oz cubes and wrapped individually in polythene with a date label. The storage time will be four to six weeks in a freezer. Dried yeast will keep for six months if stored in a tightly sealed tin in a cool place. An alternative is fast-action dried yeast, which can be added straight into the flour mix.

Fifteen grams/½ oz dried yeast is equivalent to 30g/1 oz fresh yeast. Yeast mixtures rise best if the moisture is kept in. This may be done by covering the tin with a sheet of lightly greased polythene or slipping the tin into a lightly greased polythene bag during rising.

The time the dough takes to rise in the tin varies with the temperature – about 45 minutes in a warm place – a little over an hour at room temperature. Do not over-raise yeast mixtures or they will collapse on baking.

To test if bread is cooked, tip it out of the tin and tap the bottom of the loaf – it should sound hollow. Gluten-free bread goes stale quickly, and if you are making it in bulk you should freeze it immediately after baking and cooling. Do not store bread in the refrigerator

Brown bread (*left*, see page 72); White bread (*centre*, see page 71); White scones (*above right*, see page 73); Brown scones (*below right*, see page 73)

as this accelerates staling. Slice loaves before freezing so you can defrost just as much as you need. Put the loaf in a plastic bag and seal, excluding as much air as possible. Many people find that gluten-free bread is better toasted and you can toast straight from the freezer.

Gluten-free bread will keep well in a freezer for up to six months. Thaw at room temperature for three to four hours or in a refrigerator overnight. Refresh in a hot oven for 5 minutes. Stale bread can be toasted or made into breadcrumbs and stored in an airtight container.

See also Baking and breadmaking, page 32, and Which flour to use? page 38.

Gluten-free baking powder

85g/3 oz cornflour
100g/3½ oz bicarbonate of soda
60g/2 oz cream of tartar
60g/2 oz tartaric acid (from the
chemist)

Mix all the ingredients together and pass through a fine sieve two or three times. Store in an airtight container in a dry place.

White bread See photograph, page 69

Makes 2 small loaves

Each loaf: 910Cals/3820kJ, 0 g fibre

430ml/¾ pt milk and water (half   *1 tsp granulated sugar*
and half)   *340g/12oz plain gluten-free flour**
2 tsp dried yeast or 30g/1oz fresh   *1 tsp salt*
yeast   *30g/1oz lard*

Grease two 0.5kg/1 lb loaf tins. Warm the milk and water until just comfortable to the touch. Put one-third of the milk and water in a bowl, sprinkle the dried yeast on to it and add a pinch of sugar; or, cream the fresh yeast with a pinch of sugar and a little of the warm liquid. In either case, leave to stand in a warm place for about 10 minutes until frothy.

Sift the flour and the salt, add the rest of the sugar and rub in the fat. Make a well in the centre and add the yeast and sufficient liquid to make a stiff batter. Beat, adding more milk and water as it thickens

* Tested with Aproten gluten-free flour

Date and walnut loaf (*top left*, see page 75); Banana bran bread (*top right*, see page 74); Butter cob (*bottom*, see page 74)

until you have a smooth batter that drops heavily from the spoon, adding more water, if necessary. Divide the batter between the two tins, cover with oiled polythene, or a damp cloth, and set in a warm place for 20–30 minutes or until risen to the top of the tins.

Heat the oven to 220°C/425°F/gas 7. Stand the tins on a baking sheet and bake for about 30 minutes, until well risen, firm and a light brown. Cool for a few minutes in the tin and turn on to a wire rack.

Slice and freeze if not to be used at once.

To make one large loaf allow 40–50 minutes and reduce the temperature to 200°C/400°F/gas 6 for the last 10 minutes.

Brown bread

See photograph, page 69

Makes 1 small loaf

Each slice: 70Cals/290kJ, 2g fibre

1 tsp dried yeast or 7.5g/¹/₄oz fresh yeast
¹/₂ tsp sugar
255ml/9 fl oz warm water at blood heat

225g/8oz plain gluten-free flour*
¹/₂ tsp salt
30g/1 oz soya bran

Grease a 0.5kg/1 lb loaf tin.

Dissolve the yeast and the sugar in approximately one-third of the warm water. Leave in a warm place until frothy – about 10 minutes.

Sift together the flour and salt and stir in the soya bran. Add the dissolved yeast and the rest of the water. Beat either by hand (2–3 minutes) or with an electric mixer on slow speed (1–2 minutes) until a thick smooth batter is formed. Put the batter in the loaf tin, cover with oiled polythene and stand in a warm place until the top of the batter is level with the top of the tin (normally 30–40 minutes).

Heat the oven to 230°C/450°F/gas 8. Bake on a middle shelf for 25–35 minutes or until firm. Let the bread stand in the tin for 5 minutes before removing.

To make 12 rolls, use the above recipe but add only 140–225ml/5–8 fl oz water – to make a soft dough.

* Tested with Rite-Diet gluten-free flour mix

White scones
See photograph, page 69

Makes 8

Each scone: 210Cals/880kJ, 1 g fibre

*225g/8oz self-raising gluten-free
  flour**
½ tsp salt
1 tsp gluten-free baking powder
60g/2oz hard margarine*

*60g/2oz granulated sugar
60g/2oz mixed dried fruit
  (optional)
approximately 140ml/5 fl oz milk*

Heat the oven to 200°C/400°F/gas 6. Grease a baking sheet.
  Sift flour, salt and baking powder into a bowl. Add the margarine cut into pieces and rub in until the mixture resembles breadcrumbs. Add the sugar, and fruit if used and mix to a soft dough with the milk. Roll out on a board dusted with gluten-free flour to about 1cm/½ in thick and cut into rounds with a plain cutter. Or divide into two, shape into rounds 1cm/½ in thick and mark into four. Place on the baking sheet and bake 10–15 minutes for small scones or 20–25 minutes for the larger rounds. They should be well risen and browned. Cool on a wire tray.

* Tested with Tritamyl gluten-free flour

Brown scones
See photograph, page 69

Makes 8

Each scone: 120Cals/500kJ, 4 g fibre

*280g/10 oz plain gluten-free flour**
½ tbsp gluten-free baking powder
1 tsp salt
45g/1½oz soya bran*

*60g/2oz hard margarine
1 tbsp sugar
170–225ml/6–8 fl oz milk*

Heat the oven to 200°C/400°F/gas 6. Grease a baking sheet.
  Sift together the flour, baking powder and salt into a bowl. Add the soya bran. Rub in the margarine until the mixture resembles breadcrumbs. Add the sugar. Mix to a sticky dough with the milk. Roll out on a board dusted with gluten-free flour to about 1cm/½ in thick. Cut into rounds with a plain cutter. Place on the baking sheet and bake for 15–20 minutes or until lightly browned. Cool on a wire tray and store in an airtight tin.

Alternatives
For cheese scones, omit sugar and add 60–85g/2–3oz grated hard cheese.
  For fruit scones, add 60–85g/2–3oz dried fruit with the sugar.
  For pizza base, omit sugar.

* Tested with Rite-Diet gluten-free flour mix

Butter cob

See photograph, page 70

Makes 2 loaves or 16 small rolls

Each roll: 160Cals/670kJ, 0 g fibre

450g/1 lb plain gluten-free flour
pinch salt
2 tsp gluten-free baking powder

115g/4oz butter
½ tsp sugar
280ml/½ pt milk (or more, as required)

Heat the oven to 200°C/400°F/gas 6. Dust a baking sheet with gluten-free flour. Sift the flour and baking powder into a large bowl, rub in the fat and add the sugar. Mix with sufficient milk to make a sticky dough. Knead lightly to bring it together. Form into two large cobs 2–4cm/1–1½ in thick and mark the tops with a cross.

Bake the loaves for 20 minutes and then reduce the heat to 190°C/375°F/gas 5 for 10 minutes covering with greaseproof paper if browning too quickly.

Alternatives   Make into 16 small rolls or a pizza base, using one-third of the amounts for an 18cm/7 in pizza. Bake the rolls for 15 minutes at 200°C/400°F/gas 6. For the pizza, see page 66.

Corn bread

Makes 16 slices

Each slice: 80Cals/340kJ, 0 g fibre

115g/4oz cornmeal
115g/4oz plain gluten-free flour
1 tsp salt
3 tsp gluten-free baking powder

1 tbsp brown sugar
200ml/7 fl oz milk
1 egg, grade 3
60g/2oz butter, melted

Heat the oven to 220°C/425°F/gas 7. Grease a 20cm/8 in square tin.

Sift together the cornmeal, flour, salt and baking powder. Stir in the sugar. Beat the egg lightly and add the milk and melted butter. Stir into the dry ingredients, mixing well. Pour the mixture into the tin and bake for 20–30 minutes, until lightly browned. Cool in the tin for 5 minutes and remove to a cooling rack.

Banana bran bread

See photograph, page 70

Makes 16 slices

Each slice: 160Cals/670kJ, 4 g fibre

115g/4oz soft margarine
115g/4oz soft brown sugar

1 egg, grade 1 or 2
2 large ripe bananas, mashed

225g/8oz plain gluten-free flour*
1 tsp gluten-free baking powder
1 tsp gluten-free mixed spice

85g/3oz raisins
60g/2oz soya bran
milk to mix, as necessary

Heat the oven to 180°C/350°F/gas 4. Grease a 1 kg/2 lb loaf tin and line the bottom with greaseproof paper.

Cream the margarine and sugar until light. Beat the egg, mash the bananas and gradually add to the creamed mixture. Sift together the flour, baking powder and spice, and add the dried fruit, bran and sufficient milk to form a stiff dropping mixture. Spoon into the tin, level mixture and bake in the centre of the oven for 1¼–1½ hours. Leave in the tin for 5 minutes, then remove to a cooling tray. Store in a polythene bag in a cool place. Freezes well.

This loaf can be served as a plain cake or sliced and buttered.

* Tested with Aproten gluten-free flour

Bran fruit loaf

Makes 2 small loaves

Each slice: 60Cals/250kJ, 5g fibre

400g/14oz mixed dried fruit
340ml/12 fl oz cold tea
255g/9oz plain gluten-free flour
3 tsp gluten-free baking powder

¼ tsp gluten-free mixed spice
115g/4oz soya bran
70g/2½oz brown sugar
2 eggs, grade 2, beaten

Heat the oven to 180°C/350°F/gas 4. Grease two 0.5kg/1 lb loaf tins well.

Soak the fruit in the tea for at least 30 minutes. Sift together flour, baking powder and mixed spice. Mix in the soya bran and the sugar. Add the fruit, tea and eggs and beat together well. Divide the mixture between the two loaf tins and bake for 1 hour or until brown and firm. Leave in the tin for a few minutes and then turn out on to a cooling rack.

Date and walnut loaf See photograph, page 70

Makes 16 slices

Each slice: 190Cals/800kJ, 1 g fibre

225g/8oz chopped dates
170g/6oz demerara sugar
85g/3oz margarine
grated rind 1 orange
30ml/2 tbsp orange juice

1 egg, grade 4
225g/8oz plain gluten-free flour*
1½ tsp gluten-free baking
  powder
1 tsp ground cinnamon
60g/2oz chopped walnuts

* Tested with Aproten gluten-free flour

Heat the oven to 180°C/350°F/gas 4. Grease a 1 kg/2 lb loaf tin and line the bottom with greased greaseproof paper.

Simmer the dates with 140ml/5 fl oz water in a covered pan for 15 minutes or until soft. The water should all be absorbed by the time the dates are cooked; if it tends to dry out add more. Stir in the sugar and margarine and remove pan from the heat. Add the grated orange rind and juice, beat in the egg. Sift the flour, baking powder and cinnamon together and add to the mixture. Add the walnuts. Mix well and spoon into the prepared tin. Bake for 1 hour 10 minutes–1 hour 20 minutes, until a skewer comes out clean. Cool in the tin for 5 minutes, then remove to a wire rack. Store wrapped in foil in a cool place. Serve sliced as it is, or buttered.

Canadian muffins
See photograph, page 79

Makes 6

Each muffin: 130Cals/550kJ, 0 g fibre

1 egg, grade 4	*pinch salt*
60ml/2 fl oz milk	*1½ tsp gluten-free baking powder*
15ml/1 tbsp melted butter	*15g/½oz granulated sugar*
115g/4oz plain gluten-free flour	

Heat the oven to 200°C/400°F/gas 6. Grease six muffin tins or patty tins.

Beat the egg and milk in a bowl. Add the melted butter, and stir well. Sift the gluten-free flour, salt and gluten-free baking powder together and stir in the sugar. Add the egg mixture to the dry ingredients, stirring only just enough to mix. *Do not beat* and do not mix until smooth; the batter should be coarse and stiff. Place 2 heaped teaspoonfuls in each tin. Bake for 20 minutes or until well-risen and brown.

Best served warm immediately after cooking. If the muffins are left to go cold, they can be rewarmed by being wrapped loosely in aluminium foil and heated in a hot oven (230°C/450°F/gas 8) for 5 minutes.

Alternatives   For savoury or sweet muffins add the following:
60g/2oz crisp cooked bacon pieces
  (omit sugar)
60g/2 oz grated cheese (omit sugar)
60g/2oz chopped nuts
60g/2oz any dried fruit

These should be mixed with the dry ingredients.

Russian pancakes (blini) See photograph, page 79

Makes 20

Each pancake: 40Cals/170kJ, 0 g fibre

115g/4oz buckwheat flour
45g/1½ oz Rite-Diet gluten-free
brown bread mix
1 tsp gluten-free baking powder

½ tsp bicarbonate of soda
¼ tsp salt
1 tsp sugar
340/ml/12 fl oz buttermilk or milk
soured with 5ml/1 tsp vinegar

Grease a griddle or heavy frying pan. Sift the buckwheat into a bowl with the bread mix, baking powder, bicarbonate of soda and salt – tip in any grain that remains in the sieve. Add the sugar. Add the buttermilk or soured milk to the dry ingredients, stirring to combine. Do not beat. This forms a very thin batter. Leave to stand for a few minutes.

Warm the griddle on a medium heat. Drop tablespoons of the batter carefully on to the griddle, leaving room for them to spread. They will form about 7cm/3 in pancakes. Cook for 2–3 minutes until bubbles appear on the surface. They will lift easily with a palette knife. Turn and cook for a further 2–3 minutes. Regrease the griddle or pan between additions as necessary. Pile on to a dish and keep warm. Serve at once.

These go well with breakfast dishes such as bacon, sausages, scrambled eggs. They are equally good with honey, maple syrup or jam.

Welsh griddle cakes See photograph, page 79

Makes 12

Each cake: 150Cals/630kJ, 1 g fibre

vegetable oil to grease the griddle
225g/8oz plain gluten-free flour
pinch salt
1½ tsp gluten-free baking powder
¼ tsp grated nutmeg or gluten-free mixed spice (optional)

85g/3oz hard margarine
60g/2oz granulated sugar
60g/2oz currants
1 egg, grade 2
a little milk to mix
caster sugar to dust

Grease and heat a griddle or heavy frying pan to a moderate heat. Sift the gluten-free flour, salt and gluten-free baking powder and spice, if using, into a bowl. Rub in the fat, add the sugar and currants. Beat the egg, add about a tablespoonful of milk, pour on to the dry mixture and bring together. Work into a stiff paste, adding more milk if necessary. Turn out on to a board dusted with gluten-free flour and pat or roll into a circle, not less than 0.5cm/¼ in thick.

Cut into triangles or rounds with a cutter. Lift with a palette knife on to the hot griddle. Cook each side for 4–5 minutes or until set, adjusting the heat as necessary. When cooked lift on to a piece of greaseproof paper and dust with sugar on both sides.
Serve immediately or buttered when cold.

PUDDINGS

As well as the recipes in this section, sago and tapioca are gluten-free, and fruit is an easy and healthy way to end a meal. Ready-made pie fillings, dessert mixes and ice creams may contain gluten (see also the table on page 28).

COLD PUDDINGS

Muesli

Each serving (dry): 180Cals/760kJ, 7 g fibre

60g/2oz rolled (porridge) oats
2 tbsp soya bran
2 tbsp sunflower seeds

30g/1oz chopped walnuts
30g/1oz stoned dates
30g/1oz raisins

Mix all the ingredients together. They may be mixed in a large quantity and stored in a screw-top jar. Grated eating apple or fresh or stewed fruit in season may be added, and the muesli sweetened with honey or brown sugar. Muesli can be eaten alone or with milk or gluten-free yoghurt. For those who cannot tolerate oats, substitute another tablespoon of soya bran and more sunflower seeds and add some desiccated coconut.
Muesli can also be eaten as a snack, or for breakfast.

Canadian muffins (*top left*, see page 76); Blinis (*centre*, see page 77);
Welsh griddle cakes (*bottom*, see page 77)
OVERLEAF: Baked lemon delight (*top left*, see page 89); Fruit crumble (*bottom left*, see page 87); Brown Betty (*right*, see page 88)

Pineapple cheesecake

Makes 12 slices

Each slice: 210Cals/880kJ, 0 g fibre

Base:
9 *gluten-free digestive biscuits*
60g/2oz *margarine*
30g/1oz *demerara sugar*
a little ground cinnamon (optional)

Top:
15g/½oz *powdered gelatin*
115ml/4 fl oz *pineapple juice*

170g/6oz *pineapple pieces*
2 *eggs, grade 2, separated*
85g/3oz *caster sugar*
225g/8oz *sieved cottage*
  cheese
140ml/5 fl oz *soured or double*
  cream
angelica to decorate

Grease an 18–20cm/7–8 in loose-bottomed cake tin.
To make the base, crush the biscuits. Melt the margarine and mix with the sugar, cinnamon and biscuit crumbs. Press the mixture on to the base of the tin and leave in a cool place to set.
Meanwhile, put the gelatin and the pineapple juice in a cup. Stand the cup in a pan of barely simmering water and stir until the gelatin has dissolved. Leave to cool. Cut up the pineapple into small pieces, reserving a few for decoration. In a mixing bowl, beat the egg yolks and sugar until light and thick. Add the dissolved gelatin, the cheese and the soured or double cream. Beat again and stir in the pineapple pieces. Lastly, when it is on the point of setting, fold in the stiffly beaten egg whites. Pour on to the prepared base and leave to set in the refrigerator (about 2–3 hours). Remove from the tin and slide the cake on to a serving plate. Decorate with pieces of pineapple and angelica.

Alternatives Lemon or orange cheesecake: use the grated rind and juice of two lemons or two oranges in place of the pineapple pieces and the pineapple juice.
Strawberries or raspberries (115g/4oz) can be used as a topping for a lemon cheesecake.

Sponge flan base

Makes 8 slices

Each slice: 80Cals/340kJ, 0 g fibre

2 *eggs, grade 2*
60g/2oz *caster sugar*

70g/2½oz *plain gluten-free flour*

Heat the oven to 200°C/400°F/gas 6. Grease a sponge flan tin 20cm/8 in in diameter and place on a baking sheet.

Fruit sorbet (*top and centre left*, see page 85); Pineapple cheesecake (*centre right*); Fruit and nut iced cake (*bottom*, see page 85)

Whisk the eggs and sugar together until thick and light. The mixture must leave a trail from the whisk which remains for a few seconds. Sift the flour on to the mixture and fold in very lightly with a metal spoon. Finally, fold in 15ml/1 tablespoonful of boiling water. Do not mix or beat any further. Pour the batter into the tin and bake for 15 minutes. The sponge should be firm, golden brown and springy to the touch. Leave to cool in the tin for at least 5 minutes. Ease out carefully and cool on a wire rack with the top side down.

Suggested fillings   When cold, fill with seasonal fresh fruit such as strawberries or raspberries, or any drained tinned fruit. If using fresh fruit, stew a few berries in about 140ml/5 fl oz of water to extract the flavour. Drain the juice and measure it. Take 200ml/7 fl oz of juice; blend a tablespoonful of cornflour with a little of the juice and bring the rest to the boil. Pour on to the cornflour, return to the pan and boil for 5 minutes, until it coats the back of a spoon. Sweeten to taste. Pour over the flan. If using tinned fruit, use the juice in the same way, but it may not need any extra sugar.

Lemon meringue pie

Serves 6

Each serving: 330Cals/1390kJ, 0 g fibre

Pastry base:	Filling:
125g/4oz gluten-free flour	*30g/1oz cornflour*
pinch salt	*grated rind and juice 2 lemons*
60g/2oz hard margarine	*115g/4oz granulated sugar*
1 egg, grade 4, beaten	*2 eggs, grade 2, separated*

Heat the oven to 200°C/400°F/gas 6. Make the pastry (see short-crust pastry, page 93), roll it out on a surface dusted with gluten-free flour and line a flan tin or deep pie plate 18cm/7 in in diameter. Prick the pastry all over with a fork. Line with foil and weight down the foil with dried beans or rice. Bake the pastry case for 15 minutes. Remove the foil and beans or rice and bake for a further 5 minutes to brown. Remove the pastry case from the oven and reduce the temperature to 150°C/300°F/gas 2.

Meanwhile prepare the filling. Blend the cornflour, lemon rind and juice, and 140ml/5fl oz water in a saucepan. Bring to the boil, stirring all the time, then simmer for a few minutes. Remove from the heat and add all but 2 tablespoonfuls of the sugar. Beat the egg yolks into the mixture. Pour into the pastry case. Whip the egg whites stiffly and fold in the 2 tablespoonfuls of sugar. Pile the meringue on top of the pie, covering the filling completely. Place in the cool oven for 15–20 minutes to set and brown lightly. Serve warm or cold. Do not freeze.

Fruit sorbet

See photograph, page 82

Each serving: 150Cals/630kJ, 8 g fibre

450g/1 lb soft fruit
115g/4oz granulated sugar
285ml/½ pt water

1 tsp gelatin
2 egg whites, grade 2

Turn the refrigerator on to the coldest setting or turn on the fast-freeze section of the freezer.

Purée the fruit and sieve if necessary to remove seeds. In a saucepan, dissolve the sugar in the water and bring to the boil. Boil rapidly for 5 minutes and set aside to go cold. Sprinkle the gelatin over a little water in a pan and when soaked heat gently to dissolve. Then mix together the syrup, purée and gelatin and put into a suitable container. Freeze until just mushy, about 30 minutes. Stir to remove ice crystals around the edges. Whisk the egg whites until stiff and fold into the purée. Return to the freezer for at least 2 hours. To serve allow to defrost for 10–15 minutes – the exact time will depend on the temperature of your freezer and the fruit used.

Serve with gluten-free Danish biscuits if liked (see page 99).

Raspberry mousse

Each serving: 240Cals/1010kJ, 5 g fibre

425g/15oz tin raspberries
130g/1 pkt raspberry jelly (to make
550ml/1 pt)

170g/6oz tin evaporated milk
5ml/1 tsp lemon juice

Strain the raspberries and measure the juice. Make up to 285ml/½ pt with water. Place the juice in a pan, add the jelly and warm, stirring until it is dissolved. Do not allow to boil. Leave to cool and refrigerate until it is beginning to set. Purée the raspberries. Place the evaporated milk and lemon juice in a bowl and whisk until the mixture is very thick and will hold soft peaks. Fold in the raspberry purée and the jelly. Pour into a serving dish and leave to set, preferably in a refrigerator.

Other fruit and a correspondingly flavoured jelly can be used.

Fruit and nut iced cake

See photograph, page 82

Serves 12

Each serving: 170Cals/710kJ, 1 g fibre

115g/4oz mixed dried fruit
60g/2oz maraschino cherries or
washed glacé cherries,
quartered

30ml/2 tbsp sherry
200ml/7 fl oz milk
1 tsp powdered gelatin
1 tsp powdered instant coffee

1 tsp gluten-free cocoa
60g/2oz chopped walnuts
60g/2oz caster sugar (to taste)

a few drops vanilla essence
285ml/½ pt whipping cream
chopped nuts and cherries

Turn refrigerator to lowest setting or switch on the fast-freeze section of a deep-freeze.

Mix the fruits and the sherry and leave to stand for about 30 minutes. Warm the milk and dissolve the gelatin in it. Add the coffee and cocoa. Remove from the heat and cool in a large bowl. When cold add the soaked fruit and sherry, nuts, sugar and vanilla essence. Whip the cream until it forms soft peaks, fold into the fruit mixture and turn into a bowl. Freeze for about 1 hour. Take out of the freezer and mix well with a fork to distribute the fruit evenly. Re-freeze until required.

Remove from freezer about 30 minutes before serving. Dip the bowl into hot water for a second and turn on to a serving dish. Sprinkle with the nuts and cherries.

Dutch fruit salad

Each serving: 180Cals/760kJ, 4 g fibre

225g/8oz tin pineapple pieces
60g/2oz sugar (optional)
rind 1 lemon
juice ½ lemon
340g/12oz fresh fruit, eg, apples,

plums, oranges, melon, grapes
and soft fruit
15–30ml/1–2 tbsp kirsch
chopped preserved ginger
(optional)

Drain the pineapple, saving the juice. Make the juice up to 285ml/½ pt with water or orange juice. Place in a small saucepan with the sugar. Add the lemon rind and juice. Heat gently, stirring to dissolve the sugar. Bring to the boil and simmer for 5 minutes. Leave to infuse for 20 minutes. Meanwhile prepare the fruits, cutting them into suitable sized pieces (if using bananas, slice into the salad just before serving). Pour the cooled syrup over the fruit. Stir in the kirsch, and pieces of ginger, if using. Chill in the refrigerator.

Simple ice cream

Each serving: 340Cals/1430kJ, 0 g fibre

285ml/½ pt milk
2 tbsp gluten-free custard powder
115g/4oz caster sugar
285ml/½ pt double cream, well
  chilled, or 400g/14oz tin

evaporated milk, well chilled
a few drops vanilla essence
(optional)

Turn the refrigerator to its lowest setting or switch on the fast-freeze section of a deep-freeze.

Make a custard with the milk and custard powder as directed on the packet. Add the sugar. Set aside to cool. Whip the cream or evaporated milk until very thick. Add the cold custard and mix well. Flavour if desired with vanilla essence. Pour into freezing trays and freeze until just set round the sides. Return to a bowl and whisk. Replace in the freezing trays and freeze until hard. Store in a deep freeze. Remove from the freezer 30 minutes before required and keep in the refrigerator until served.

May be flavoured by adding instant coffee or other gluten-free flavourings to the milk during the making of the custard.

HOT PUDDINGS

Baked custard

Each serving: 170Cals/710kJ, 0 g fibre

2 eggs
30g/1oz granulated sugar
550ml/1 pt milk

a few drops vanilla essence
(optional)
grated nutmeg

Heat the oven to 170°C/325°F/gas 3. Grease a 1 1/2 pt pie dish. Beat the eggs lightly with the sugar. Warm the milk to blood heat and pour on to the eggs and sugar. Mix well, adding vanilla essence, if using. Pour the custard into the pie dish. Grate a little nutmeg on top. Place the pie dish in a tin of water in the oven; the water should come about halfway up the sides of the pie dish – this prevents the custard curdling. Bake for 1 hour or until the custard sets. Serve warm or cold.

Baked apples go well with this and can be baked at the same time.

Fruit crumble

See photograph, page 80

Serves 6

Each serving: 360Cals/1510kJ, 6 g fibre

450g/1 lb raw fruit, eg, plums,
cooking apples, gooseberries or
rhubarb
115g/4oz brown sugar, according
to taste; some fruits need more
than others

30g/1oz soya bran
85g/3oz hard margarine
60g/2oz walnuts or toasted
hazelnuts, finely chopped
(optional)
30g/1oz demerara sugar

Topping:
140g/5oz gluten-free flour

Heat the oven to 180°C/350°F/gas 4. Grease a 1 1/2 pt pie dish.

Prepare the fruit, mix with the brown sugar and place in the pie dish. Mix the gluten-free flour and soya bran and rub in the margarine until the mixture resembles fine breadcrumbs. Stir in the nuts, if using, and demerara sugar. Tip over the fruit and press gently down. Place in the centre of the oven. Bake for about 1 hour, until the fruit is tender. If the top browns too quickly reduce the heat to 170°C/325°F/gas 3. Serve hot with gluten-free custard or cold with cream.

Alternatives   A little dried fruit or chopped ginger may be added to the raw fruit, and mixed spice or cinnamon to the demerara sugar.

Brown Betty
See photograph, page 81

Each serving: 440Cals/1850kJ, 4 g fibre

60g/2oz margarine
8 gluten-free digestive biscuits,
  crushed, or 85g/3oz dried
  gluten-free breadcrumbs
140g/5oz brown sugar

450g/1 lb cooking apples
juice 1 lemon
1 tsp ground cinnamon
1/4 tsp ground nutmeg
grated rind 1/2 lemon

Heat the oven to 180°C/350°F/gas 4. Grease a 1.5 1/2½ pt oven-proof dish.

Melt the margarine and add the bread or biscuit crumbs and 30g/1oz of the brown sugar. Mix well. Line the bottom of the dish with a third of this mixture. Peel, core and slice the apples very thinly and put in a bowl. Sprinkle with the lemon juice, and mix in the remaining brown sugar, spices, lemon rind and 30ml/2 tablespoonfuls of water. Stir well. Place half this mixture on top of the crumbs in the dish. Cover with a further third of the crumbs, repeat the fruit layer and top with the remainder of the crumbs. Press down lightly. Cover with greased greaseproof paper and bake in the centre of the oven for about 40 minutes or until the apples are nearly soft. Increase the heat to 200°C/400°F/gas 6, remove the greaseproof paper and cook for a further 15 minutes until the top is crisp and brown.

An alternative   Add a tablespoonful of dried mixed fruit to each layer of apples.

Old-fashioned rice pudding

Each serving: 240Cals/1010kJ, 3 g fibre (bran included)

700ml/1¼ pt milk
60g/2oz pudding rice
15g/½oz soya bran (optional)
45g/1½oz granulated sugar

2 pieces lemon rind
15g/½oz margarine
½ tsp grated nutmeg

Heat the oven to 170°C/325°F/gas 3. Grease a 1 1/2 pt pie dish.
Warm the milk. Put the rice, bran, if using, sugar, lemon rind and margarine in the dish and pour the milk over. Stir to dissolve the sugar. Add the nutmeg and stir again. Bake for 2–3 hours, stirring once or twice during the first hour, and then leave undisturbed for the remaining time.

Baked lemon delight

See photograph, page 80

Each serving: 280Cals/1180kJ, 0 g fibre

60g/2oz soft margarine
60g/2oz granulated sugar
2 eggs, grade 4, separated

1 tbsp gluten-free flour
grated rind and juice 1 large lemon
285ml/½ pt milk

Heat the oven to 180°C/350°F/gas 4. Grease a 1 1/2 pt pie or soufflé dish.
Cream the margarine and sugar together until very light. Beat in the egg yolks and then the flour, lemon rind and juice. Beat well. Mix in the milk carefully, do not worry if it curdles a little. Beat the egg whites until they just hold peaks and fold in carefully. Pour into the greased dish and bake for 45 minutes. It should be slightly risen and firm on top. Serve hot or cold.

Orange pudding

Each serving: 320Cals/1340kJ, 0 g fibre

60g/2oz soft margarine
60g/2oz caster sugar
1 egg, grade 2
grated rind 1 orange
85g/3oz plain gluten-free flour

pinch salt
¼ tsp gluten-free baking powder
15–30ml/1–2 tbsp milk
3 tbsp orange marmalade
(optional)

Grease a 0.5 l/1 pt pudding basin. In a mixing bowl, cream the margarine and sugar until light. Beat in the egg and orange rind. Sift together the gluten-free flour, salt and gluten-free baking powder and fold into the creamed mixture. Add milk as required to form a soft dropping consistency. Spread the marmalade, if using, on to the bottom of the basin and spoon in the mixture. Cover first with greased greaseproof paper, and then with foil, folding and twisting it over the rim of the basin to keep out the steam. Place in a steamer or in a covered pan containing water halfway up the sides of the basin. Bring to the boil and steam for 50–60 minutes. Carefully add more boiling water as necessary. Serve hot with gluten-free custard or marmalade sauce.

Bread and butter pudding

Each serving: 550Cals/2310kJ, 2 g fibre

60g/2oz butter or margarine
6 slices gluten-free bread
4 tbsp thick marmalade (optional)
1 medium cooking apple, grated or thinly sliced

85g/3oz brown sugar
60g/2oz raisins
1 tsp ground cinnamon (optional)
2 eggs, grade 2
430ml/³/₄ pt milk

Heat the oven to 180°C/350°F/gas 4. Grease a 1.5 l/2½ pt pie dish.

Butter each slice of bread and spread with marmalade, if using. Make a layer of the bread and marmalade in the bottom of the dish. Cover with half the apple, half the sugar and half the raisins, and some cinnamon, if using. Repeat once and end with a layer of bread and marmalade, buttered side down. Dot with a little more butter and a sprinkling of sugar. Beat the eggs and milk together and pour over. Press down and leave to stand at least 30 minutes. Bake for about 45 minutes or until the custard is set and the top is crispy. Serve hot or cold.

Christmas pudding

Each serving: 270Cals/1130kJ, 3 g fibre

30g/1oz plain gluten-free flour
⅛ tsp salt
¼ tsp gluten-free mixed spice
⅛ tsp bicarbonate of soda
grated rind ½ lemon
60g/2oz cooking apple, grated
60g/2oz brown sugar
30g/1oz chopped almonds
60g/2oz sultanas

60g/2oz currants
30g/1oz raisins
30g/1oz chopped mixed peel
45g/1½oz gluten-free shredded suet
70g/2½oz gluten-free breadcrumbs
1 egg, grade 2
45–60 ml/3–4 tbsp milk

Grease a 0.5kg/1 lb pudding basin. Sift the flour, salt, mixed spice and bicarbonate of soda into a large mixing bowl. Add the lemon rind, apple, sugar, almonds, dried fruit, shredded suet and bread-crumbs. Mix well. Beat the egg with the milk. Gradually stir into the mixture, which should form a soft dropping consistency: if it is too stiff add a little more milk. Spoon into the basin, cover with greased greaseproof paper and then with foil. Place in a steamer or in a covered pan containing water halfway up the sides of the basin. Bring to the boil and steam for 5 hours, topping up with boiling

Profiteroles (*top*, see page 96); Almond fruit pastries (*centre*, see page 94); Brandy snaps (*bottom*, see page 104)

water as necessary. Allow to cool. Cover with new foil or a cloth and seal well.

When ready for use, steam for 1–1½ hours and serve.

This pudding improves with keeping and can be stored for up to a year. If it becomes dry moisten with a little cider or milk before re-steaming.

PASTRIES, BISCUITS AND SMALL CAKES

Gluten-free pastry is very good. If it cracks when it is being rolled out it is because it is too dry. Always add a few teaspoonfuls more water than you think necessary. Do not roll out too thinly: it should be about 0.5cm/¼ in thick or more. If you are not going to use the pastry immediately, wrap it in a plastic bag or foil to prevent it drying out, and store in a refrigerator or freezer.

See also Baking and breadmaking, page 32, and Which flour to use? page 38.

Shortcrust pastry

Sufficient for 12 small tarts or 1 x 18cm/7 in single pie crust

115g/4 oz pastry: 950Cals/3990kJ, 0 g fibre

115g/4oz plain gluten-free flour　　*30g/1oz hard margarine*
pinch salt　　*1 egg, grade 4*
30g/1oz white vegetable fat
(from the refrigerator)

Heat the oven to 200°C/400°F/gas 6.

Sift the flour and salt into a bowl. Cut the fats into the flour and

---

Coconut squares (*top and centre left*, see page 106); Plain oaten biscuits (*top right and bottom left*, see page 100); Danish biscuits (*centre right*, see page 99); Nutty squares (*bottom right*, see page 102)

then, using your fingertips, rub in lightly until the mixture resembles dry breadcrumbs. Beat the egg with 15ml/1 tablespoonful cold water. Sprinkle it over the crumb mixture and mix lightly. This should form a pliable but not sticky dough. If you are not using the pastry immediately, make a wetter dough as it tends to dry out on standing. To roll out, lightly dust a board and a rolling pin with gluten-free flour, place the dough on the board and roll firmly, lifting and flouring underneath to prevent sticking. Do not roll less than 0.5cm/¼ in thick. Use as required.

NB   There is no need to grease tins or dishes when using shortcrust pastry. It will not stick if you use at least half the quantity of fat to flour. Prick well before filling to prevent the pastry rising. You will need pastry made with 170g/6oz flour for a top and bottom crust tart 18cm/7 in diameter.

Rich sweet crust pastry

Sufficient for 24 small tarts or 2×18cm/7 in single pie crusts

225g/8oz pastry: 1930Cals/8110kJ, 0 g fibre

225g/8oz plain gluten-free flour *60g/2oz caster sugar*
pinch salt *1 egg, grade 2*
115g/4oz butter or hard margarine *5–10ml/1–2 tsp lemon juice*
* (from the refrigerator)*

There is no need to grease the tins to be used.
 Sift the flour and salt into a bowl. Cut the fat into small pieces and rub into the flour until the mixture resembles fine breadcrumbs. Stir in the sugar. Beat the egg with the lemon juice and sprinkle over the crumb mixture. Bring together gently and knead into a ball. Add a few drops of water if the pastry is too dry. It should form a soft pliable dough. Heat the oven to 200°C/400°F/gas 6. Wrap the pastry in foil and chill for 30 minutes in the refrigerator. Do not roll out less than 0.5cm/¼ in thick. Use as required.

Almond fruit pastries See photograph, page 91

Makes 6 wedges

Each wedge: 220Cals/920kJ, 2 g fibre

60g/2oz soft margarine *60g/2oz plus a little extra soft*
60g/2oz ground rice * brown sugar*
60g/2oz plain gluten-free flour *30g/1oz ground almonds*
1 large eating apple, unpeeled *flaked almonds to decorate*

Heat the oven to 220°C/425°F/gas 7. Grease an ovenproof plate or tin 20cm/8 in diameter.

Blend the margarine, ground rice and flour together with a fork. Grate half the apple and mix it in with 60g/2oz of the sugar and the ground almonds. Knead into a ball. Press out on the plate. Thinly slice the rest of the apple and arrange in circles on the pastry, working towards the centre. Sprinkle with a little more sugar and decorate with the flaked almonds. Bake for 20 minutes, or until browned. Cut into wedges and serve warm or cold.

For a change, mix some cinnamon with the brown sugar sprinkled on the top.

Welsh cheese cakes

Makes 12

Each cake: 230Cals/970kJ, 0 g fibre

*½ quantity rich sweet crust pastry
  (see opposite)*

Filling:
*raspberry jam
45g/1½oz soft margarine
45g/1½oz caster sugar*

*1 egg, grade 4
30g/1oz plain gluten-free flour
60g/2oz ground rice
½ tsp gluten-free baking powder
a few drops vanilla essence
icing sugar*

Heat the oven to 200°C/400°F/gas 6.

Roll and cut out the pastry into 6cm/2½ in circles. Line twelve patty tins with the pastry and place a small teaspoonful of jam in each. In a bowl, cream the margarine and sugar until very light and beat in the egg. Sift together the flour, ground rice and baking powder. Fold into the creamed mixture with the vanilla essence. Divide equally between the twelve tarts. Bake for 15 minutes, then reduce the heat to 190°C/375°F/gas 5 for a further 5 minutes. Cool on a wire tray. Dust with icing sugar to serve.

Apple cinnamon shortcake

Makes 12 pieces

Each piece: 150Cals/630kJ, 2 g fibre

*150g/5oz plain gluten-free flour
1 tsp gluten-free baking powder
½ tsp cinnamon
30g/1 oz soya bran
85g/3oz hard margarine*

*85g/3oz plus 1 tbsp caster sugar
1 egg, grade 4, beaten
170g/6oz cooking apple, peeled,
  cored and thinly sliced*

Heat the oven to 180°C/350°F/gas 4. Grease an 18cm/7 in square or a 20cm/8 in round tin and line with greaseproof paper. Sift the flour, baking powder and cinnamon together into a bowl. Mix in the bran, and rub in the margarine. Stir in 85g/3oz of the caster sugar. Work most of the egg into the mixture and knead until smooth, adding more egg if the pastry is too dry to roll out. Divide the pastry in half and roll out one half to fit the tin. Line the base of the tin with the pastry. Place a layer of apple over the top and press down. Roll out the other half of the pastry and place over the apple. Press well down and brush with a little milk. Mark with a fork and sprinkle with the extra tablespoon of sugar. Bake for 30–40 minutes or until lightly browned. Leave to cool in the tin. Lift out, peel off the paper and cut the shortcake into pieces. Will keep for several days, wrapped, in a refrigerator.

An alternative Substitute ½ teaspoonful ground ginger for the cinnamon and spread a thick layer of ginger marmalade in place of the apple.

Mince pies

Makes 12

Each pie: 230Cals/970kJ, 0 g fibre

1 quantity rich sweet crust pastry (see page 94)
340g/12oz gluten-free mincemeat

egg white or milk to glaze
icing sugar

Heat the oven to 200°C/400°F/gas 6.

Roll out the pastry, cut out twelve circles using a 6cm/2½ in pastry cutter and line the patty tins. Cut the tops using a cutter one size smaller. Fill with the gluten-free mincemeat. Moisten the edges with water and cover with the tops, pressing the edges well down to seal. Make a slit in each top to let out the steam. Brush the tops with egg white or milk. Bake for 15–20 minutes or until golden brown. Cool on a wire rack and dust with icing sugar before serving.

Choux pastry for profiteroles or chocolate éclairs
See photograph, page 91

Makes 15 éclairs or puffs

Each: 140Cals/590kJ, 0 g fibre

85g/3oz plain gluten-free flour
pinch salt
45g/1½oz hard margarine
2 eggs, grade 4 (not larger)
140ml/4 fl oz double or whipping cream, whipped until stiff

Chocolate glacé icing:
2 tsp gluten-free cocoa
170g/6oz icing sugar

Chocolate sauce:

45g/1½oz plain gluten-free cooking chocolate, broken into pieces	*pinch salt*
	60g/2oz granulated sugar
	a few drops vanilla essence
1 tsp cornflour	*15g/½oz margarine*

Heat the oven to 220°C/425°F/gas 7. Grease a large baking sheet. Sift the flour and salt together. Put 140ml/5 fl oz water and the margarine in a small saucepan over heat. When the margarine has melted, bring to the boil. Tip in the flour all at once, remove pan from the heat and beat until smooth. Beat one egg in until the mixture is smooth and glossy. Repeat with the second egg. It should form a stiff paste. For profiteroles, place teaspoonfuls on the baking sheet. For éclairs, pipe 7cm/3 in lengths, using a 2cm/1 in nozzle. Bake for 25–30 minutes in the middle of the oven. Do not open the door for at least 25 minutes. When the buns are well risen, browned and crisp remove from the oven. Cut a slit in each to allow the steam to escape and leave to cool on a wire rack. When cold fill with whipped cream. Cover with chocolate glacé icing (see below). Alternatively, the filled buns may be piled on a dish and chocolate sauce poured over them.

To make the icing, dissolve the cocoa in a little warm water (15–30ml/1–2 tablespoonfuls) and gradually add to the icing sugar. The icing should be thick enough to coat the back of a spoon: if needed add water or sugar to adjust. Use at once.

To make the chocolate sauce, add 115ml/4 fl oz water to the chocolate in a small saucepan and melt over a low heat. Mix the cornflour and salt with a little water to make a smooth cream. Bring 85ml/3 fl oz water to the boil and pour on to the blended cornflour, stirring. Return to the pan and bring back to the boil, stirring continuously. Add the chocolate and the sugar and cook for 4–5 minutes, stirring and beating. Finally, stir in the vanilla essence and the margarine, leave to cool and pour over the buns.

Shortbread

Makes 15 fingers

Each finger: 110Cals/460kJ, 0 g fibre

140g/5oz plain gluten-free flour	*115g/4oz butter (not straight from the refrigerator, but not soft)*
30g/1oz ground rice	
60g/2oz granulated sugar plus a little for dusting	

Heat the oven to 180°C/350°F/gas 4.

Mix the flour and ground rice in a large bowl and stir in the sugar. Place the butter in one piece in the bowl and work in with one hand, kneading until the mixture binds together and becomes smooth. Turn on to a board dusted with gluten-free flour and shape into a rectangle.

Roll out to a strip 30×7cm/12×3 in and about 1cm/½ in thick. Nip the edges between thumb and forefinger as you go along to form a pattern. Prick well and dust with a little granulated sugar. Cut into fingers 1.5–2cm/¾–1 in wide. Use a palette knife to place well apart on an ungreased baking tray and bake in the middle of the oven for 20–30 minutes or until pale golden. Cool on the baking sheet. Store in an airtight tin when cold.

Basic biscuit mixture

Makes 36 biscuits

Each biscuit: 70Cals/290kJ, 1 g fibre

170g/6oz gluten-free flour　　　*170g/6oz caster sugar*
60g/2oz soya bran　　　　　　　*1 egg, grade 3*
115g/4oz soft margarine　　　　*milk to mix, as necessary*

any of the following may be added to the mixture:
30–60g/1–2oz chopped nuts, candied peel, ginger pieces, chopped glacé cherries, grated orange or lemon rind, or gluten-free chocolate chips

Heat the oven to 190°C/375°F/gas 5. Grease two or three baking sheets.

Sift flour into a bowl and add the other ingredients. Work together with a wooden spoon and then knead lightly to form a ball. Add a little milk if the dough will not hold together. Turn on to a board dusted with gluten-free flour and roll into a sausage not more than 30cm/12 in long. Wrap it in greaseproof paper and refrigerate for 30 minutes. When firm cut into 0.5cm/¼ in slices with a sharp knife and lift on to a baking sheet, leaving space for the slices to spread. Bake for 15–20 minutes, until well browned. Cool on a wire rack. Store in an airtight tin. If you wrap the dough in foil it freezes very well.

May be decorated with glacé icing and an almond or a cherry, or coated with melted gluten-free chocolate.

Cheese biscuits

Makes 20

Each biscuit: 40Cals/170kJ, 0 g fibre

60g/2oz well-flavoured cheese,　　*dash cayenne pepper (optional)*
*　grated*　　　　　　　　　　　　*½ tsp salt*
85g/3oz plain gluten-free flour　　*60g/2oz hard margarine*

Grease a baking sheet.

Mix the cheese, flour, cayenne pepper, if using, and salt in a bowl and rub the fat into them. Dust your hand with gluten-free flour and knead mixture into a ball. Wrap the dough in cling-film or grease-proof paper and refrigerate for 30 minutes. Heat the oven to 190°C/375°F/gas 5. Roll out on to a board dusted with gluten-free flour to 0.5cm/¼ in thick. Prick well and cut into small biscuits. Put the biscuits on the baking sheet and bake for 10–15 minutes until pale gold – do not overcook or the cheese may become bitter. Cool on a wire rack and store in an airtight tin.

Crisp crystal biscuits

Makes 20

Each biscuit: 90Cals/380kJ, 2 g fibre

140g/5oz plain gluten-free flour	*115g/4oz hard margarine*
60g/2oz ground rice	*1 egg, grade 4, separated*
85g/3oz caster sugar	*a little demerara sugar*
60g/2oz soya bran	

Heat the oven to 180°C/350°F/gas 4. Grease two baking sheets.
 Mix the flour, ground rice, sugar and bran. Rub in the margarine until the mixture resembles fine breadcrumbs. Add the egg yolk and knead until smooth. Wrap the dough in greaseproof paper and refrigerate for 30 minutes. Roll out to 0.5cm/¼ in thickness. Use a 7cm/3 in pastry cutter to cut out the biscuits and place them well apart on the prepared sheet. Brush the biscuits with the lightly beaten egg white and sprinkle with demerara sugar. Bake for 15 minutes or until golden brown. Leave to cool a little and then remove to a cooling rack. Store in an airtight tin.
 For variety add a little cinnamon to the sugar before sprinkling it over the biscuits.

Danish biscuits

See photograph, page 92

Makes 30

Each biscuit: 100Cals/420kJ, 2 g fibre

225g/8oz plain gluten-free flour	*2–3 drops almond essence*
60g/2oz soya bran	*1 egg yolk, grade 4, beaten*
170g/6oz slightly salted butter	*1 egg white, lightly beaten*
115g/4oz granulated sugar	*a little granulated sugar*
60g/2oz chopped almonds	*30 flaked almonds*

Heat the oven to 180°C/350°F/gas 4. Grease two baking sheets.
 Mix the flour and bran and lightly rub in the butter. It will be difficult so do not try to form 'fine breadcrumbs', just break it up. Add the sugar, almonds and essence and rub again to mix evenly.

Bind together with the egg yolk. Turn on to a board lightly dusted with gluten-free flour. Form into a sausage and work into a smooth roll, not more than 30cm/12 in long. Wrap in greaseproof paper and chill in the refrigerator until firm, at least 30 minutes. Roll into walnut-sized balls, press flat and place well apart on the baking sheets. Brush with the lightly beaten egg white and sprinkle a little sugar on each. Decorate with an almond flake. Bake until golden brown, about 20 minutes. Leave on the trays for 5 minutes to set. Cool on a wire tray and store in an airtight tin.

New Zealand biscuits

Makes 30

Each biscuit: 90Cals/380kJ, 1 g fibre

140g/5oz hard margarine
1 tbsp golden syrup – measure with
* a warmed spoon*
60g/2oz brown sugar
115g/4oz self-raising gluten-free
* flour**

115g/4oz (porridge) oats
1 tsp ground ginger, or to taste
60g/2oz desiccated coconut
½ tsp bicarbonate of soda

Heat the oven to 170°C/325°F/gas 3. Grease two baking sheets. Slowly melt the margarine, golden syrup and sugar in a large pan. Remove from the heat. Mix together the flour, oats, ginger and coconut. Dissolve the bicarbonate of soda in 15ml/1 table-spoonful hot water, add to the pan and then add the dry ingredients. Cool for 10–15 minutes or until the mixture becomes stiff. Take walnut-sized pieces and pat into balls in your hands. Place on the prepared trays, flatten slightly, leaving room for them to spread a little. Bake for 20–30 minutes, or until golden brown. Cool on a wire tray. The biscuits keep well stored in an airtight tin.

* Tested with Tritamyl gluten-free flour

Plain oaten biscuits   See photograph, page 92

Makes 24

Each biscuit: 70Cals/290kJ, 1 g fibre

85g/3oz rolled (porridge) oats
115g/4oz medium oatmeal
85g/3oz gluten-free flour
½ tsp salt

60g/2oz hard margarine
140ml/5 fl oz (or as required) milk
* soured with 1 tsp vinegar*

Heat the oven to 190°C/375°F/gas 5. Dust one or two baking sheets with gluten-free flour.

Mix the dry ingredients together in a large bowl. Rub in the margarine and mix with sufficient milk to make a soft sticky dough. Place on a board lightly floured with gluten-free flour. Roll out to 0.5cm/¼ in thick. Prick well. Cut into squares with a sharp knife or fluted potato chipper. Place on baking sheets and bake until lightly browned, 15–20 minutes. Remove to a cooling tray. Store in an airtight tin.

A plain biscuit to eat with cheese or jam. They keep well.

To make a sweet version of this biscuit add 60g/2oz demerara sugar.

Oat crunchies

Makes 20

Each biscuit: 90Cals/380kJ, 1 g fibre

115g/4oz hard margarine   *115g/4oz light brown sugar*
130g/4½oz rolled (porridge) oats

Heat the oven to 190°C/375°F/gas 5. Grease a 28×18cm/11×7 in baking tin and line it with greased greaseproof paper.

Gently melt the margarine, do not allow it to brown. Mix the oats and the sugar in a bowl. Pour the melted fat on to the mixture and mix well. Turn on to the baking sheet and press it down firmly with your hands. Bake in the centre of the oven for 15–20 minutes or until pale gold, turning the tray after 10 minutes to ensure even cooking. Cut into squares whilst still hot. Leave in the tin to cool. When cold store in an airtight tin.

Flapjacks

Makes 14

Each flapjack: 150Cals/630kJ, 1 g fibre

115g/4oz soft brown sugar   *15ml/1 tbsp golden syrup –*
115g/4oz margarine   *measure with a warmed spoon*
170g/6oz rolled (porridge) oats   *¾ tsp ground ginger*

Heat the oven to 150°C/300°F/gas 2. Grease a Swiss roll tin (28×18cm/11×7 in).

Melt the sugar and margarine in a saucepan. Stir in the oats, syrup and ginger. Press the mixture evenly into the prepared tin. Bake for 40 minutes or until golden brown. Allow to cool slightly and mark into fingers with a sharp knife.

The flapjacks may be stored in an airtight tin for up to 1 week.

Nutty squares

See photograph, page 92

Makes 24

Each square: 100Cals/420kJ, 1 g fibre

115/4oz margarine
200g/7oz rolled (porridge) oats
60g/2oz raisins or sultanas
60g/2oz demerara sugar

60g/2oz chopped peanuts (not salted)
1 egg, grade 4, beaten

Heat the oven to 180°C/350°F/gas 4. Grease 1 28×18cm/11×7 in shallow tin and line with greased greaseproof paper. Melt the margarine. Mix all the dry ingredients in a large bowl, add the beaten egg and then the melted margarine. Mix well. Press firmly into the tin. Bake for 40–45 minutes or until well browned. Mark into squares while warm. Cool in the tin. Store in an airtight tin.

Ginger snaps

Makes 24 biscuits

Each biscuit: 90Cals/380kJ, 0 g fibre

225g/8 oz plain gluten-free flour*
2 tsp gluten-free baking powder
pinch salt
1 tsp ground ginger
115g/4 oz caster sugar

85g/3 oz margarine
60ml/4 tbsp golden syrup – measure with a warmed spoon
1 egg, grade 3, beaten

Heat the oven to 180°C/350°F/gas 4. Grease four baking sheets.
   Sift together the flour, baking powder, salt and ground ginger. Stir in the sugar. Melt the margarine and golden syrup together and add to the dry ingredients with the beaten egg. Mix together well.
   Place small teaspoonfuls of the mixture in mounds on the baking sheets.
   Bake in the centre of the oven for about 15 minutes. Leave to cool slightly, then transfer to a wire rack.

* Tested with Rite-Diet gluten-free flour mix

Date and nut squares

Makes 15

Each square: 140Cals/590kJ, 3 g fibre

85g/3oz hard margarine
115g/4oz stoned dates, chopped
60g/2oz soft brown sugar
30g/1oz walnuts, chopped
30g/1oz glacé cherries, chopped

60g/2oz Rice Krispies
30g/1oz soya bran
115g/4oz gluten-free plain chocolate

Grease an 18cm/7 in square cake tin and line the bottom with greased greaseproof paper.

Place the margarine and the dates in a pan and heat slowly. Stir in the sugar and cook for a few minutes. Mix in the walnuts, cherries, Rice Krispies and bran. Press the mixture firmly into the prepared tin. Melt the chocolate in a basin over hot water, allow to cool slightly and spread over the biscuit mixture. Chill in a refrigerator until set. Cut into fingers.

Peanut fingers

Makes 12

Each biscuit: 120Cals/500kJ, 2 g fibre

60g/2oz soft margarine
60g/2oz brown sugar
1 egg, grade 3 or 4, beaten
½ tsp gluten-free baking powder
¼ tsp ground cinnamon

85g/3oz plain gluten-free flour
30g/1oz soya bran
60g/2oz gluten-free salted peanuts
milk to mix, as necessary

Heat the oven to 180°C/350°F/gas 4. Grease an 18cm/7 in square tin.

Cream the margarine and sugar until light and fluffy. Beat the egg and blend into the creamed mixture. Sift the baking powder, cinnamon and flour together and fold into the mixture. Add the bran, the peanuts and a little milk if the mixture is too dry. Spread in the prepared tin and bake on the middle shelf until well browned, 20–30 minutes. Mark into fingers and leave to cool. Turn on to a wire rack while still warm. When cold store in an airtight tin; they will keep for about a week.

Chocolate nut fingers

Makes 24

Each finger: 130Cals/550kJ, 1 g fibre

170g/6oz plain gluten-free
  chocolate
115g/4oz walnuts, coarsely
  chopped
60g/2oz margarine

115g/4oz desiccated coconut
85g/3oz caster sugar
grated rind ½ orange
1 egg

Heat the oven to 180°C/350°F/gas 4. Grease a Swiss roll tin 28×18cm/11×7 in and at least 3cm/1 in deep, and line the base with a strip of greaseproof paper.

Break the chocolate into pieces and melt in a bowl over a pan of hot water. Stir in the chopped nuts. Spread the chocolate nut mixture evenly over the base of the tin. Leave to cool. Put the remaining ingredients into a bowl and beat until the mixture forms a smooth paste. Spread evenly over the chocolate. Bake for 25 minutes or until golden brown. Leave until cold and then cut into slim fingers.

Florentines

Makes 24

Each biscuit: 80cals/340kJ, 1 g fibre

60g/2oz butter
60g/2oz granulated sugar
2 tsp whipping cream
30g/1oz glacé cherries, chopped
30g/1oz chopped mixed peel

60g/2oz almonds, finely chopped
60g/2oz almonds, flaked
115g/4oz gluten-free plain chocolate

Heat the oven to 180°C/350°F/gas 4. Cover two large baking sheets with non-stick baking paper.

Melt the butter and sugar in a saucepan. Stir in the cream and remove from the heat. Blend in the rest of the ingredients except the chocolate. Place teaspoonfuls of the mixture well apart on the prepared baking sheets. Bake for 10–15 minutes or until golden brown. Melt the chocolate in a basin over hot water. When the biscuits are cold turn them over and spread the underside of each biscuit with a teaspoonful of chocolate. Leave to harden and store in an airtight tin.

Brandy snaps   See photograph, page 91

Makes 20

Each snap: 90Cals/380kJ, 0 g fibre

30ml/2 tbsp golden syrup –
  measure with a warmed spoon
60g/2oz hard margarine
60g/2oz granulated sugar
60g/2oz plain gluten-free flour

1/2 tsp ground ginger
5ml/1 tsp brandy or rum essence
225ml/8 fl oz whipping cream,
  whipped until stiff

Heat the oven to 170°C/325°F/gas 3. Grease well two baking sheets.

Put the golden syrup, margarine and sugar in a pan and heat gently. Stir until the sugar has dissolved and the margarine is melted – do not boil. Sift together the flour and ginger and beat into the syrup until smooth. Stir in the brandy or rum essence. Place 4–6 heaped teaspoonfuls, well spaced, on to each baking sheet. Bake one sheet at a time for 10 minutes each, turning the tray round after 5 minutes to ensure even cooking. When the biscuits are golden brown, remove the tray and allow to cool for about 30 seconds. When the biscuits are just beginning to set, lift them with a palette knife and fold over the greased handle of a wooden spoon. Mould round the handle and rest on the baking sheet to cool. Slip the curled brandy snap on to a cooling tray. If the biscuits set too quickly, return to the oven for a minute or two to soften and try again. After a little practice it is quite simple – using two wooden spoons makes it easier. Fill with whipped cream to serve but store unfilled in an airtight tin.

NB Brandy snaps are difficult to make but can be perfected with practice. This recipe makes excellent very thin, crisp snaps; here are some points to aid success.
- The baking sheets must be very well greased – use margarine or oil.
- Measure the ingredients very carefully, especially the syrup if you are making a smaller quantity.
- At first, bake just two snaps at a time for better, quicker removal from the baking tray. As you become more skilled you can bake up to four at a time.

Melting moments

See photograph, page 109

Makes 20

Each biscuit: 70Cals/290kJ, 0 g fibre

115g/4oz hard margarine
45g/1¹/₂oz icing sugar
*60g/2oz self-raising gluten-free flour**

60g/2oz cornflour
3–4 drops vanilla essence

Heat the oven to 170°C/325°F/gas 3. Cover two baking sheets with greased greaseproof paper or non-stick baking paper.
 Cream the margarine with the sugar until very light. Sift the flours together and work into the creamed mixture with the vanilla essence until very smooth. Pipe small biscuits on to the prepared trays or, with gluten-free floured hands, form walnut-sized pieces into balls and flatten slightly with the back of a fork. Bake for about 20 minutes until pale gold. Allow to cool on a wire rack. Store in an airtight tin.

Alternatives
Sandwich together with a thick butter icing.
 Add a few drops of very strong coffee to the mixture and sandwich with the coffee-flavoured cream icing.
 For Viennese biscuits, pipe the mixture in swirls and decorate with a piece of glacé cherry.

*Tested with Juvela gluten-free mix

Coconut squares

See photograph, page 92

Makes 9

Each square: 230Cals/970kJ, 2 g fibre

60g/2oz soft margarine
30g/1oz granulated sugar
1 egg, grade 4
85g/3oz plain gluten-free flour
pinch salt
30g/1oz soya bran

2 tbsp raspberry jam

Topping:
85g/3oz desiccated coconut
85g/3oz granulated sugar
1 egg, grade 4

Heat the oven to 180°C/350°F/gas 4. Grease an 18cm/7 in square tin and line with greaseproof paper.

Cream the margarine and sugar until light and fluffy. Beat in the egg. Sift the flour and salt together and mix in. Stir in the bran. Spread this mixture over the base of the prepared tin. Warm the jam and spread on top. Mix the topping ingredients in a small bowl, spread on top of the jam, and mark the top lightly with a fork. Bake for 30–40 minutes or until lightly browned and firm. Leave to cool in the tin, then cut into squares. Store in a cool place.

Coconut and cherry chocolate slices

Makes 12

Each slice: 210Cals/880kJ, 2 g fibre

85g/3oz soft margarine
60g/2oz granulated sugar
1 egg, grade 2
115g/4oz desiccated coconut
30g/1oz gluten-free flour

60g/2oz glacé cherries, chopped
115g/4oz gluten-free plain
*   chocolate*
15g/¹⁄₂oz margarine

Heat the oven to 180°C/350°F/gas 4.

Grease an 18cm/7 in square tin and line the bottom with greased greaseproof paper.

Cream the soft margarine and sugar until light. Beat in the egg. Mix the desiccated coconut with the flour and fold it in. Add the glacé cherries. Smooth into the prepared tin and bake for 20–30 minutes or until firm and brown. Leave in the tin to go cold. Melt the chocolate and 15g/¹⁄₂oz margarine in a small bowl placed over hot water, allow to cool and pour it over. As the chocolate sets mark with wavy lines with a fork and score into fingers. Store in a cool place.

Almond macaroons

Makes 15

Each macaroon: 50Cals/210kJ, 1 g fibre

1 egg white
70g/2½oz caster sugar

70g/2½oz ground almonds
2 drops almond essence

Heat the oven to 180°C/350F/gas 4. Cover a baking sheet with non-stick baking paper.

Whisk the egg white until frothy but not too stiff. Fold in the sugar, ground almonds and essence. Take walnut-sized pieces, roll quickly and lightly into balls (dip hands in cold water if the mixture becomes too sticky). Place on the baking sheet, leaving room for the macaroons to spread. Bake for 20–25 minutes or until pale golden. Allow to cool on the paper. Lift off when cold and store in an airtight container.

One tablespoonful of the ground almonds may be omitted and 1 tablespoonful ground rice used in its place.

Spicy doughnuts See photograph, page 109

Makes 9

Each doughnut: 350Cals/1470kJ, 0 g fibre

For coating:
115g/4oz granulated sugar
1–2 tsp grated nutmeg

1 egg, grade 3 or 4
115g/4oz granulated sugar
115ml/4 fl oz milk

45g/1½ oz margarine
340g/12 oz plain gluten-free flour
2 tsp gluten-free baking powder
¼ tsp salt
¼ tsp ground cinnamon
¼ tsp ground nutmeg
vegetable oil for frying

Put a sheet of absorbent paper on a baking sheet on which to drain the doughnuts. Mix 115g/4oz granulated sugar and 1–2 tsp grated nutmeg on a sheet of greaseproof paper. A fish slice and a carving fork are useful to slip the doughnuts into the oil and lift them out.

Beat the egg and whisk in the sugar and the milk. Melt the margarine and beat it in. Sift the dry ingredients together and fold into the egg and milk mixture. Mix to form a soft dough. Knead lightly to form a ball. Wrap in greaseproof paper and chill for 30 minutes until firm. Press the dough into a piece about 1cm/½ in thick on a board dusted with gluten-free flour. Cut with a plain 5cm/2 in cutter and use a 1cm/½ in cutter to make a hole in the centre. Heat the oil in a deep-frying pan until hot. Test by dropping in a cube of gluten-free bread, which should brown in 30 seconds. Cook the doughnuts in the hot oil until light brown. Drain and turn in the sugar and nutmeg. Serve at once.

Chelsea buns

Makes 8

Each bun: 300Cals/1260kJ, 1 g fibre

115ml/5fl oz milk
½ tsp sugar
1 tsp dried yeast
255g/9oz Rite-Diet gluten-free
*   white bread mix*
1 tsp ground cinnamon
½ tsp grated nutmeg
30g/1oz hard margarine

30g/1oz margarine
85g/3oz currants
30g/1oz sugar

Glacé icing:
170g/6oz icing sugar, sifted
2–3 drops vegetable oil

Heat the oven to 200°C/400°F/gas 6. Grease a small baking sheet. Warm the milk to blood heat. Dissolve half a teaspoonful of sugar in the milk and sprinkle the dried yeast on the top. Leave in a warm place to froth for about 10 minutes. Sift the bread mix and spices into a large bowl and rub in the hard margarine. Add the yeast and milk mixture and bind together with a knife. Knead lightly. Cover with oiled polythene and leave in a warm place for about 30 minutes or until doubled in bulk. Turn on to a board dusted with gluten-free flour and roll out to a 25cm/10in square. Melt the 30g/1oz margarine and brush it over the dough. Sprinkle with the currants and sugar and roll up firmly like a Swiss roll. Moisten the edge with water to seal. Cut into eight slices and place cut side down on the greased baking sheet. Cover again with oiled polythene or a damp cloth. Put in a warm place and leave to prove for 20 minutes or until well risen. Bake near the top of the oven for 15 minutes. Reduce the heat to 190°C/375°F/gas 5 for a further 5–10 minutes. Remove the buns from the oven and cool on a rack. Make the glacé icing by gently heating 30ml/2tbsp water in a saucepan. Gradually beat in the icing sugar and oil. The icing should be smooth, glossy and of a pouring consistency, so add a little more water if necessary. When the buns are cool, dribble a little icing over each.

These buns are best eaten the day they are made, but they do freeze well. Allow them to go cold and then freeze promptly.

Spicy doughnuts (*top left*, see page 107); Coffee-sandwiched melting moments (*top right*, see page 105); Chelsea buns (*bottom*)

CAKES

Cakes cooked with gluten-free flour turn out very well, but here are a few points to aid success. Check the cake ten to fifteen minutes before the final baking time: if it is browning too quickly, lower the temperature and/or cover it with greaseproof paper. To test if a fruit cake or tea bread is cooked, push a skewer or knitting needle into the middle – when it is done the skewer will come out clean. To test a sponge cake, push the centre lightly with a finger and it should spring back. Leave all cakes in the tin for at least five minutes after cooking and then cool on a wire rack. If a cake cracks during baking it is usually because it is cooking too quickly.

Cakes are best frozen straight after baking and cooling. They can be decorated first (take care that the decorations are gluten-free) but keep longer if undecorated. Storage time for decorated cakes is four to six weeks, undecorated cakes about three months. Thaw cakes at room temperature. The thawing time depends on how thick the cake is – one hour for small cakes, two to three hours for larger cakes.

See also Baking and breadmaking, page 32, and Which flour to use?. page 38.

Victoria sandwich

Makes 10 slices

Each slice: 220Cals/920kJ, 0 g fibre

115g/4oz soft margarine
115g/4oz caster sugar
2 eggs, grade 4 or 3
1/4 tsp vanilla essence (optional)
115g/4oz plain gluten-free flour
pinch salt
1/2 tsp gluten-free baking powder
a little milk
jam
whipped cream

Heat the oven to 190°C/375°F/gas 5. Grease two 18cm/7 in sandwich tins and line the bottoms with greased greaseproof paper.

Cream the margarine and sugar together, beat in the eggs one at a time, and add the vanilla essence, if using. Sift the flour, salt and baking powder together into a bowl and fold into the creamed mixture, adding a little milk if necessary to make a soft-dropping consistency. Divide between the two tins and bake for about 20 minutes or until golden brown and firm. Cool on a wire rack. Sandwich together with jam and cream.

Ginger ring cake (*top*, see page 116); Victoria sandwich (*centre*); Rich fruit cake (*bottom*, see page 119)

Alternatives
Use different flavourings, eg, orange rind, lemon rind or coffee essence.
Add 60g/2oz mixed dried fruit and bake in prepared bun cases for 15–20 minutes. Makes about 12.

Apple cake

Makes 8 slices

Each slice: 310Cals/1300kJ, 1 g fibre

140g/5oz soft margarine
85g/3oz granulated sugar
1 egg, grade 2
½tsp salt
200g/7oz plain gluten-free flour
½tsp gluten-free baking powder

Filling:
2 large cooking apples, peeled,
  cored and sliced
1 tsp cinnamon
85g/3oz granulated sugar

Heat the oven to 170°C/325°F/gas 3. Grease an 18cm/7 in square tin or a 20cm/8 in round tin and line with greaseproof paper.
Cream the margarine and sugar until light. Beat in the egg. Sift together the flour, salt and baking powder and fold into the mixture. Spread three-quarters on to the base of the prepared tin. Cover with the sliced apple, and sprinkle with the cinnamon and sugar. Place teaspoonfuls of the remaining mixture on top. Bake in the centre of the oven until the cake is set and the apple is soft, about 1–1½ hours. Sprinkle with icing sugar and serve warm or cold as a dessert cake.

Almond cake

Makes 12 slices

Each slice: 220Cals/920kJ, 4 g fibre

115g/4oz blanched almonds
140g/5oz caster sugar
3 eggs, grade 3
60g/2oz plain gluten-free flour
pinch salt

½ tsp gluten-free baking powder
45g/1½oz soya bran
85g/3oz margarine
15ml/1tbsp kirsch or Amaretto
  liqueur

Heat the oven to 170°C/325°F/gas 3. Grease two 18–20cm/7–8 in sandwich tins and line the bottoms with greased greaseproof paper.
Grind the almonds finely in a blender or food processor. Place the sugar and eggs in a large bowl and beat thoroughly until light and thick. Sift together the flour, salt and baking powder, add the bran and almonds and fold in lightly with a metal spoon. Melt the margarine. Fold the liqueur and margarine lightly into the batter. Pour into the two cake tins. Bake for 25–30 minutes or until the cake is firm. Cool for 5 minutes in the tin. Loosen the sides and turn gently on to a wire rack.

These cakes can be sandwiched together with apricot jam and dusted with icing sugar or served as a dessert with stewed apricots.

Golden cake

Makes 10 slices

Each slice: 140Cals/590kJ, 1 g fibre

70g/2½oz gluten-free instant potato powder (not granules)
1 tsp gluten-free baking powder
85g/3oz margarine
60ml/4 tbsp golden syrup – measure with a warmed spoon

85g/3oz soft brown sugar
grated rind 1 orange
30ml/2 tbsp orange juice
2 eggs, grade 4, separated
butter icing (optional)

Heat the oven to 180°C/350°F/gas 4. Grease a 16–18cm/6–7 in sandwich tin and line it with greased greaseproof paper.

Place the instant potato and baking powder in a bowl and mix well. Heat the margarine, syrup, sugar, orange rind and juice in a pan, stirring to dissolve the sugar – do not boil. Pour the mixture on to the instant potato and beat well. Beat the egg yolks into the mixture. Whisk the egg whites until very stiff and lightly fold into the mixture. Pour into the tin and bake for 35–45 minutes. If browning too quickly, cover with a sheet of greaseproof paper after 30 minutes. Cool in the tin for 5 minutes then remove to a wire rack. When cold, store in an airtight tin in a cool place. Ice with butter icing if desired. Best eaten within two days.

Marmalade cake

Makes 16 slices

Each slice: 160Cals/670kJ, 0 g fibre

115g/4oz soft margarine
115g/4oz soft brown sugar
2 eggs, grade 4
225g/8oz plain gluten-free flour
4 tbsp coarse-cut marmalade

1 tsp gluten-free baking powder
pinch salt
¼ tsp gluten-free mixed spice
30g/1oz chopped mixed peel
30ml/2 tbsp milk to mix

Heat the oven to 170°C/325°F/gas 3. Grease a 0.5kg/1 lb loaf tin and line the bottom with greased greaseproof paper.

Cream the margarine and sugar very well, until light. Beat in the eggs one at a time with a teaspoonful of the flour. Add the marmalade and beat in. Sift the remaining flour, baking powder, salt and spice and fold in gradually. Mix in the peel and sufficient milk to form a fairly soft mixture. Spoon into the tin and bake in the middle of the oven for 1¼–1½ hours. If the cake browns too quickly place a sheet of greaseproof paper over it. Leave to cool in the tin for 5 minutes. Lift out and cool on a wire rack. Keeps well stored in a cool place.

Seed cake

Makes 12 slices

Each slice: 90Cals/380kJ, 0 g fibre

85g/3oz soft margarine
85g/3oz granulated sugar plus
extra for sprinkling
115g/4oz plain gluten-free flour
pinch salt

1/4 tsp gluten-free baking powder
1 egg, grade 1 or 2
30g/1oz chopped mixed peel
1 1/2 tsp caraway seeds

Heat the oven to 180°C/350°F/gas 4. Grease an 18cm/7 in sandwich tin and line the bottom with greased greaseproof paper.

Cream together the margarine and the sugar. Sift together the flour, salt and baking powder. Beat the egg and add to the creamed mixture. Fold in the flour and add the peel and 1 teaspoonful caraway seeds. If the mixture is too stiff add a little cold milk, to form a soft dropping consistency. Spoon into the tin and level. Sprinkle extra sugar and seeds on top. Bake for 35–45 minutes or until firm and lightly browned.

Carrot cake

Makes 12 slices

Each slice: 230Cals/970kJ, 3 g fibre

225g/8oz carrots, finely grated
6 eggs, grade 2 or 3, separated
225g/8oz granulated sugar
225g/8oz ground almonds

1/4 tsp ground cinnamon
30g/1oz ground rice
grated rind 1 lemon
15–30ml/1–2 tbsp lemon juice

Heat the oven to 190°C/375°F/gas 5. Grease two 18cm/7 in tins and line the bottoms with greased greaseproof paper.

Put the egg yolks in a bowl with the sugar and beat until light and creamy. Mix the ground almonds, cinnamon and ground rice together and blend well. Fold the almond mixture and carrots into the creamed mixture with the lemon rind and juice. Finally, beat the egg whites until stiff and fold them in very lightly to form a soft dropping consistency. Pour the batter into the two tins and bake for 20 minutes. Reduce the oven temperature to 180°C/350°F/gas 4 if the cakes are browning too quickly, and bake for a further 20–25 minutes. Remove from the tins and cool on a wire tray. Keep in a refrigerator.

A dessert cake. Can be sandwiched together with apricot jam and served with tinned or stewed apricots or peaches.

Swiss roll

Makes 8 slices

Each slice: 110Cals/460kJ, 0 g fibre

2 eggs, grade 2	*15ml/1 tbsp boiling water*
60g/2oz caster sugar	*warm jam*
*70g/2½oz plain gluten-free flour**	*icing sugar*

Heat the oven to 220°C/425°F/gas 7.

Line a Swiss roll tin (18×28cm/7×11 in) with greased greaseproof paper.

Prepare the sponge as for sponge flan (see page 83). Pour the mixture into the prepared tin and bake near the top of the oven for 7–10 minutes. It is a thin cake and bakes quickly. Do not overbake. Have ready a sheet of greaseproof paper with sugar sprinkled on it. Turn the cake over quickly on to the paper. If the edges are crisp trim them off. Spread with the warm jam. Roll up the cake, using the paper to help and keeping the roll as tight as possible. Leave to cool on a wire rack. Dust with icing sugar.

Alternatives For a chocolate swiss roll, substitute 1 tablespoonful gluten-free cocoa for 1 tablespoonful gluten-free flour. Sift the flour and cocoa together and proceed as before.

To fill with whipped cream or butter cream: roll the cake up whilst warm with a sheet of greaseproof paper inside. Cool. When cold unroll very gently and spread with the chosen filling. Re-roll not too tightly.

Cover with gluten-free chocolate butter cream to make a chocolate log for Christmas.

* Tested with Rite-Diet gluten-free flour mix

Chocolate cake

Makes 12 slices

Each slice: 210Cals/880kJ, 0 g fibre

115g/4oz soft margarine	*30g/1oz gluten-free cocoa*
140g/5oz caster sugar	*a few drops vanilla essence*
2 eggs, grade 2	*pinch salt*
115g/4oz plain gluten-free flour	*1 tsp gluten-free baking powder*

Heat the oven to 180°C/350°F/gas 4. Grease two 18cm/7 in sandwich tins and line the bottoms with greased greaseproof paper. Cream the margarine and sugar together until light. Beat in the eggs one at a time, adding a little flour if necessary to prevent curdling. Add the vanilla essence and fold in the rest of the flour sifted together with the salt, baking powder and cocoa. Divide the mixture between the two tins and bake for 25–35 minutes or until firm. Remove the cakes from the tins and cool on wire racks.

These cakes can be served separately or sandwiched together with whipped cream, butter cream or jam. They can be iced with chocolate or coffee icing.

Chocolate munchy cake

Makes 12 slices

Each slice: 190Cals/800kJ, 2 g fibre

*115g/4oz plain gluten-free
  chocolate
85g/3oz margarine
1 egg yolk, grade 4, beaten
115g/4 oz gluten-free digestive
  biscuits, crushed*

*60g/2oz raisins or sultanas
30g/1oz glacé cherries, chopped
  (optional)
60g/2oz flaked almonds, toasted*

Grease a loose-bottomed flan or sandwich tin and line the bottom with greased greaseproof paper. Break the chocolate into pieces and place, with the margarine, in a basin over hot water to soften. Cool slightly. Add the egg to the chocolate mixture. Stir in the biscuit crumbs, fruit and nuts. Turn the mixture into the prepared tin and smooth the top. Mark top into slices when nearly set. Chill for at least 1 hour before serving.

Ginger ring cake   See photograph, page 110

Makes 12 slices

Each slice: 170Cals/710kJ, 4 g fibre

*225g/8oz plain gluten-free flour
2 tsp gluten-free baking powder
pinch salt
1 tsp cinnamon
2 tsp ground ginger
85g/3oz sugar*

*60g/2oz soya bran
15ml/1 tbsp golden syrup –
  measure with a warmed spoon
85g/3oz margarine
1 egg, grade 2 or 3, beaten
200–225ml/7–8 fl oz milk*

Heat the oven to 180°C/350°F/gas 4. Grease a ring tin 20cm/8 in diameter or a tin 18cm/7 in square and line the bottom with greased greaseproof paper. Sift the flour, baking powder and spices into a bowl and add the sugar and bran. Melt the syrup and margarine and add to the dry ingredients. Add the egg to the mixture with enough milk to form a thick pouring batter. Beat until smooth and pour into the prepared tin. Bake on the middle shelf for 35–45 minutes or until the cake is well risen and firm. Leave it to cool in the tin for 5 minutes. Turn on to a cooling rack and wrap in foil when cold. Keep

2–3 days before use for the cake to mature. This cake keeps well.

May be iced with a lemon-flavoured glacé icing and decorated with crystallized ginger.

Ginger cake

Makes 16 slices

Each slice: 180Cals/760kJ, 1 g fibre

340g/12oz plain gluten-free flour
½ tsp gluten-free baking powder
pinch salt
½ tsp ground ginger
30g/1oz soya bran
115g/4oz butter or margarine

115g/4oz granulated sugar plus a
little for sprinkling
2 eggs, grade 2
115g/4oz preserved ginger,
drained and chopped
milk to mix, as necessary

Heat the oven to 180°C/350°F/gas 4. Grease an 18cm/7 in round tin or a large 1kg/2lb loaf tin and line the bottom with greased greaseproof paper.

Sift together the flour, baking powder, salt and ground ginger and mix in the bran. Cream together the butter or margarine and sugar and beat in the eggs one at a time. Fold in the dry ingredients together with the chopped ginger. Add about 75ml/5 tablespoonfuls milk. The mixture should drop off the spoon when shaken gently. Pour into the prepared tin. Sprinkle sugar over the top. Bake for 1¼–1½ hours or until well risen, brown and firm. Cool on a wire rack. Wrap in foil and store in an airtight tin. This cake keeps for a week or two.

Sticky gingerbread

Makes 12 squares

Each square: 240Cals/1010kJ, 0 g fibre

225g/8oz plain gluten-free flour*
pinch salt
2 tsp ground ginger
1 tsp gluten-free mixed spice
1 tsp bicarbonate of soda
60g/2oz soft brown sugar
115g/4oz margarine

90ml/6 tbsp black treacle –
measure with a warmed spoon
30ml/2 tbsp golden syrup –
measure with a warmed spoon
140ml/5 fl oz milk
2 eggs, grade 3 or 4, beaten

Heat the oven to 150°C/300°F/gas 2. Grease a 15×23cm/6×9 in cake tin and line the bottom with greased greaseproof paper.

Sift together the flour, salt, ginger, mixed spice and bicarbonate of soda. Stir in the sugar. Melt the margarine, treacle and syrup gently

* Tested with Rite-Diet gluten-free flour mix

together. Gradually beat in the milk. Allow to cool and add the eggs. Stir the treacle mixture into the dry ingredients. Pour into the cake tin and bake for about 1¼ hours, until firm.

Parkin

Makes 12 pieces

Each piece: 140Cals/590kJ, 7 g fibre

115g/4oz soya bran
60g/2oz plain gluten-free flour
1 tsp gluten-free baking powder
1 tsp ground ginger
60g/2oz hard margarine
60g/2oz brown sugar

30ml/2 tbsp black treacle – measure
  with a warmed spoon
75ml/5 tbsp golden syrup – measure
  with a warmed spoon
1 egg, grade 3 or 4, beaten

Heat the oven to 170°C/325°F/gas 3. Grease an 18cm/7 in square shallow tin and line with greaseproof paper.

Mix together the soya bran, flour, baking powder and ginger. Melt the margarine over a low heat and add the sugar, treacle and syrup, stirring until the sugar is dissolved. Add to the dry ingredients with the egg. Mix to a batter that drops easily from the spoon. Pour into the prepared tin; bake for about 45 minutes or until firm. When cool wrap in foil and, ideally, keep for a few days before eating. Keeps well stored in a cool place.

Boiled fruit cake

Makes 16 slices

Each slice: 150Cals/630kJ, 1 g fibre

140g/5oz dark brown sugar or
  molasses sugar
140ml/5 fl oz milk
60g/2oz margarine
85g/3oz dried mixed fruit
115g/4oz ground rice

85g/3oz cornmeal
85g/3oz soya flour
1 tsp gluten-free mixed spice
1 tsp gluten-free baking powder
1 egg, grade 4, beaten

Heat the oven to 180°C/350°F/gas 4. Grease a 1 kg/2 lb loaf tin.

Heat the sugar, milk, margarine and dried fruit together in a pan but do not boil. Stir until the sugar is dissolved; then leave to cool slightly. Sift all the dry ingredients together into a bowl. Add the fruit mixture and the egg. Mix well. Spoon into the greased loaf tin and level the mixture. Bake on the middle shelf for about 40 minutes. If it is browning too quickly, lower the heat to 170°C/325°F/ gas 3. Cool in the tin. This cake keeps well, stored in an airtight tin.

Rich fruit cake

See photograph, page 110

Makes 16 slices

Each slice: 250Cals/1050kJ, 2 g fibre

140g/5oz hard margarine
140g/5oz soft brown sugar
10ml/2 tsp black treacle – measure
  with a warmed spoon
225g/8oz plain gluten-free flour
½ tsp gluten-free baking powder

1 tsp gluten-free mixed spice
3 eggs, grade 3 or 4
340g/12oz mixed dried fruit
85g/3oz glacé cherries, chopped
60g/2oz ground almonds
30–60ml/2–4 tbsp milk

Heat the oven to 170°C/325°F/gas 3. Grease and line with two layers of greaseproof paper an 18cm/7 in square cake tin or 20cm/8 in round cake tin.

Cream the margarine, sugar and treacle until soft. Sift together the flour, baking powder and mixed spice. Beat in the eggs one at a time with a teaspoonful of flour, beating well each time. Fold in half the sifted flour. Then fold in the dried fruit and chopped cherries mixed with the rest of the flour and the ground almonds. The mixture should be of a heavy dropping consistency; if it is too stiff add 30–60ml/2–4 tablespoonfuls milk. Spoon into the prepared tin and bake for 1½ hours in the middle of the oven. Then lower the oven temperature to 150°C/300°F/gas 2, cover the top with two sheets of greaseproof paper and cook for a further 1–1½ hours, until a skewer comes out clean. Cool on a wire rack and when cold wrap, with its greaseproof paper, in foil. Store in a cool place. Allow several days at least to mature.

If this cake is to be used as a Christmas cake, bake with butter and keep for one month well-wrapped and stored in a cool place. One week before the cake is required, unwrap and turn it upside down. Prick the bottom and dribble brandy into it. Cover with gluten-free marzipan and ice as desired.

SAUCES

Tinned, packet or bottled sauces, gravy mixes and brownings, may contain gluten. Use cornflour to thicken. Many recipes use cornflour anyway; but if you are substituting it for ordinary flour you will need about two-thirds as much.

White sauce

Total: 350Cals/1470kJ, 0 g fibre

4 tsp cornflour
285ml/½ pt milk
knob of margarine

salt and freshly ground black
pepper

In a basin, blend the cornflour to a smooth cream with a little milk. Heat the remaining milk with the margarine until boiling and pour on to the cornflour, stirring well. Return the mixture to the pan and bring to the boil, stirring continuously with a wooden spoon. Simmer for 1–2 minutes. Season to taste. If making one of the variations below, stir in the extra ingredients and heat through.

Cheese sauce

Total: 590Cals/2480kJ, 0 g fibre

60g/2oz grated cheese
¼ tsp gluten-free prepared mustard

Mushroom sauce

Total: 480Cals/2020kJ, 0 g fibre

60g/2oz mushrooms, finely sliced and fried

Parsley sauce

Total: 350Cals/1470kJ, 0 g fibre

½ tbsp finely chopped fresh parsley

Fresh tomato sauce

Total: 1150Cals/4830kJ, 9 g fibre

60ml/4tbsp vegetable oil
1 medium onion, very finely
  chopped
60g/2oz bacon, diced
1 clove garlic, crushed (optional)
1 small carrot, chopped
340g/12oz tomatoes, skinned and
  chopped
60ml/4 tbsp gluten-free tomato
  purée

170ml/6 fl oz gluten-free stock or
  water
2 tbsp cornflour
1 bay leaf
2 cloves
4 black peppercorns
pinch basil
1 tbsp brown sugar
½ tsp salt
15ml/3 tsp lemon juice

Heat the oil in a large heavy saucepan. Add the onion, bacon, garlic, if using, and carrot. Cover the pan and fry gently for about 6 minutes. Shake the pan frequently to prevent sticking. Stir in the tomatoes and the tomato purée. Add the stock or water. Blend the cornflour with a little cold water and add to the mixture. Cook, stirring continuously, until the sauce boils and thickens. Add the rest of the ingredients. Cover and simmer for about 40 minutes, stirring frequently. Sieve the sauce, taste and adjust the seasoning.
  Serve hot or cold. Store in a screw-top jar in the refrigerator.

Quick tomato sauce

Total: 420Cals/1760kJ, 3 g fibre

30g/1oz margarine
1 small onion, peeled and grated
1 small apple, peeled and grated
90ml/6 tbsp gluten-free tomato
  purée

salt and freshly ground black
  pepper
¼ tsp sugar
2 tsp cornflour
285ml/½ pt water

Melt the margarine in a pan and fry the onion and apple for a few minutes until soft. Add the tomato purée, seasoning and sugar. Blend the cornflour with a little water to make a smooth cream and stir into the mixture in the pan. Finally, add the remaining water and bring to the boil, stirring continuously until smooth and thick. Simmer gently for about 10 minutes. Adjust the seasoning. Serve warm.

Barbecue sauce

Total: 730Cals/3070kJ, 1 g fibre

60g/2oz margarine
1 medium onion, finely chopped
1 clove garlic, crushed
1 tbsp prepared gluten-free English
  mustard

30ml/2 tbsp vinegar
large pinch cayenne pepper
2 tbsp brown sugar
1 thick slice lemon

30ml/2 tbsp Worcestershire sauce　　*60ml/4 tbsp gluten-free tomato purée*

Melt the margarine in a small saucepan and fry the onion and garlic for a few minutes, until soft but not brown. Stir in the mustard, vinegar, cayenne pepper, sugar, lemon and 140ml/5fl oz water. Bring to the boil and simmer for 15 minutes, stirring occasionally. Add the Worcestershire sauce and tomato purée, stir and simmer for another 5 minutes. Remove the lemon and serve.

Spanish sauce

Each 15ml tablespoon: 110Cals/460kJ, 0 g fibre

1 quantity mayonnaise (see page 44)
60 ml/4 tbsp gluten-free tomato purée
4 tbsp finely chopped pimiento
salt and freshly ground black pepper

Combine all the ingredients. Store in the refrigerator.

Sauce tartare

Each 15ml tablespoon: 100Cals/420kJ, 0 g fibre

1 quantity mayonnaise (see page 44)
1 tbsp chopped fresh parsley
4 tbsp capers, finely chopped
4 tbsp gherkins, finely chopped

Mix all the ingredients together. Store in the refrigerator.

Curry sauce

Total: 830Cals/3490kJ, 20 g fibre

15ml/1 tbsp vegetable oil
1 onion, finely chopped
1 clove garlic, crushed
1½ tsp cornflour
4–6 tbsp gluten-free curry powder
285ml/½ pt gluten-free stock or water
1 small apple, coarsely grated
30–60g/1–2oz desiccated coconut (optional)
1 tbsp currants (optional)
15ml/1 tbsp lemon juice
salt and freshly ground black pepper
60ml/2 fl oz top of the milk

Heat the oil in a saucepan and fry the onion and garlic for a few minutes, until soft but not brown. Sprinkle in the cornflour and curry powder, stir, and cook for a little longer. Gradually blend in the stock or water, and, stirring continuously, bring to the boil. Cover and simmer for about 20 minutes, stirring occasionally. Add the apple, coconut and currants, if using, lemon juice and seasoning, stir in the top of the milk and heat through.

USEFUL ADDRESSES

UNITED KINGDOM
The Coeliac Society of the United Kingdom
PO Box No 220
High Wycombe
Bucks. HP11 2HY

NB The services of the Coeliac Society are available only to people medically diagnosed as having coeliac disease or dermatitis herpetiformis. A stamped addressed envelope must be sent with all correspondence requiring a reply.

There are branches of the Society throughout the country.

AUSTRALIA

Australian Council of Coeliac Societies
and
Coeliac Society of NSW
PO Box 271
Wahroonga 2076

Coeliac Society of Queensland
31 Claret Street
Carseldine 4034

Coeliac Society of Western Australia
PO Box 219
Mount Lawley 6050

Coeliac Society of South Australia
15 Liverpool Crescent
Salisbury East 5109

Coeliac Society of Victoria
PO Box 22
Chadstone Centre 3148

NEW ZEALAND

Contact
Mrs B. Serjeant
9 Judith Place
Green Bay
Auckland

SOUTH AFRICA

Contact
Mrs M. Kaplan
91 Third Avenue
Percelia
Johannesburg 2192

INDEX

Page numbers in *italic* refer to the illustrations.

alcohol, 29, 31, 35
almonds: almond cake, 112–13
  almond fruit pastries,
    94–5; *91*
  almond macaroons, 107
apples: almond fruit pastries,
    94–5; *91*
  apple cake, 112
  apple cinnamon shortcake,
    95–6
  brown Betty, 88; *81*

bacon: bacon and lentil soup,
    41
  liver and bacon hotpot, 53
baked custard, 87
baking, 32, 68, 93, 111
baking powder, 32, 71
banana bran bread, 74–5; *70*
barbecue sauce, 121–2
beans, 45
beef: beef casserole, 52
  chilli con carne, 54–5
  meat loaf, 54; *57*
  steak and kidney pudding,
    53
beer, 29, 31
beverages, 29
biscuits, 95–107
blini, *see* Russian pancakes
bran, 34
bran fruit loaf, 75
brandy snaps, 104–5; *91*
bread, 32, 68–74
bread and butter pudding,
    90
brown Betty, 88; *81*
butter beans: casserole, 62
  chicken with mushrooms
    and, 61
butter cob, 74; *70*

cakes, 85–6, 95, 111–19
calories, 34–5
Canadian muffins, 76; *79*
carrot cake, 114
celery: cream of celery soup,
    40; *47*
cereals, 26, 27–8
cheese: cheese biscuits, 98
  cheese sauce, 120

lentil roast, 62
  Mediterranean baked
    courgettes, 62
  mushroom and cheese
    flan, 65
  pizza, 66
  spaghetti cheese in tomato
    sauce, 66
cheesecake, pineapple, 83; *82*
Chelsea buns, 108; *109*
cherry: coconut and cherry
    chocolate slices, 106
chicken with mushrooms and
    butter beans, 61
children: coeliac disease, 12,
    13, 14
  gluten-free diet, 21, 26,
    37
chilli con carne, 54–5
chocolate: chocolate cake,
    115–16
  chocolate munchy cake,
    116
  chocolate nut fingers,
    103–4
  coconut and cherry
    chocolate slices, 106
  Florentines, 104
choux pastry, 96–7
Christmas pudding, 90–3
coconut: coconut and cherry
    chocolate slices, 106
  coconut squares, 106; *92*
cod: fishcakes, 50; *58*
  fisherman's pie, 46
coeliac disease, 8–19
Coeliac Society, 23
communion wafers, 31
corn bread, 74
courgettes: courgette and red
    pepper flan, 65; *60*
  kidney bean and
    mushroom salad with,
    43–4; *48*
  Mediterranean baked
    courgettes, 62
crisp crystal biscuits, 99
cucumber raita, 44
curry: curry sauce, 122
  korma gosht, 51–2
  vegetable curry, 63
custard, baked, 87

dairy products, 26, 27
Danish biscuits, 99–100; *92*
dapsone, 20
dates: date and nut squares,
    102–3
  date and walnut loaf, 75–6;
    70
dermatitis herpetiformis
    (DH), 19–21
doughnuts, spicy, 107; *109*
drugs, gluten content, 31
Dutch fruit salad, 86

eating out, 36
éclairs, 96–7
eggs, 26, 27

fats, 29, 34–5
fertility, 22, 23
fibre, 34, 35
fish, 26, 27, 46–51
fishcakes, 50; *58*
fisherman's pie, 46
flans, savoury, 65
flapjacks, 101
Florentines, 104
flour, 32, 33, 38, 68
fondue, meat, 52
freezing, 32, 38, 68, 93, 111
French dressing, 44
French onion soup, 41; *47*
fruit, 26, 28
fruit and nut iced cake, 85–6;
    82
fruit cake, boiled, 118
  rich, 119; *110*
fruit crumble, 87–8; *80*
fruit salad, Dutch, 86
fruit sorbet, 85; *82*

ginger: ginger cake, 117
  ginger ring cake, 116–17;
    110
  ginger snaps, 102
  parkin, 118
  sticky gingerbread, 117–18
gluten, 10–12, 18–20
gluten-free foods, 27–30, 33
golden cake, 113
griddle cakes, Welsh, 77–8;
    79

haddock, smoked: kedgeree, 50–1
herrings in oatmeal, 49
HLA antigens, 13, 14, 20

ice cream, 86–7
intestine, small, 8–10, 11–12, 18, 19; *9, 10, 11, 12*

jejunal biopsy, 16–17, 20
jacket potatoes, 61

kedgeree, 50–1
kidney beans: chilli con carne, 54–5
kidney bean, courgette and mushroom salad, 43–4; *48*
korma gosht, 51–2

lamb: korma gosht, 51–2
lamb stew with dumplings, 56; *57*
stuffed peppers, 55–6; *57*
lemon: baked lemon delight, 89; *80*
lemon meringue pie, 84
lentils, 45
bacon and lentil soup, 41
lentil roast, 63
life insurance, 23–4
liver: country pâté, 51
liver and bacon hotpot, 53–4

macaroons, almond, 107
mackerel: baked stuffed mackerel, 49; *59*
smoked mackerel pâté, 49–50; *58*
Maggie's salad, 42; *48*
marmalade cake, 113–14
mayonnaise, 44
meat, 26, 27, 46, 51–61
meat fondue, 52
meat loaf, 54; *57*
melting moments, 105; *109*
mince pies, 96
minestrone soup, 41–2; *47*
mousse, raspberry, 85
muesli, 78
muffins, Canadian, 76; *79*
mushrooms: bacon and mushroom flan, 65
chicken with butter beans and, 61
kidney bean and courgette salad with, 43–4; *48*

mushroom and cheese flan, 65
mushroom sauce, 120

New Zealand biscuits, 100
nuts, 29
nutty squares, 102; *92*

oats, 11, 30
oat crunchies, 101
plain oaten biscuits, 100–1; *92*
onion: French onion soup, 41; *47*
orange pudding, 89

pancakes, 67–8; *60*
Russian pancakes (blini), 77; *79*
parkin, 118
parsley sauce, 120
pasta salad, 43; *48*
pastry, 64, 93–4, 96–7
pâté: country pâté, 51
smoked mackerel pâté, 49–50; *58*
peanuts: nutty squares, 102; *92*
peanut fingers, 103
peas: green pea soup, 39
peppers: courgette and red pepper flan, 65; *60*
Mediterranean baked courgettes, 62
stuffed peppers, 55–6; *57*
pilaff, vegetarian, 64
pineapple cheesecake, 83; *82*
pizza, 66; *60*
pork in cider, 55
potatoes, 46
fisherman's pie, 46
jacket potatoes, 63
pork in cider, 55
potato salad, 44
pregnancy, 22–3
processed foods, 30–1
profiteroles, 96–7; *91*
puddings, 28, 78–93
pulses, 26, 27, 45

raising agents, 29, 68, 71
raspberry mousse, 85
rice, 11, 45
kedgeree, 50–1
rice pudding, 88–9
stuffed peppers, 55–6; *57*
vegetarian pilaff, 64
rice bran, 34

Russian pancakes (blini), 77; *79*

salad dressings, 44–5
salads, 42–4
sauces, 33, 120–2
savoury flans, 65–6
scones, 73; *69*
seed cake, 114
shortbread, 97
shortcrust pastry, 93–4
sorbet, fruit, 85; *82*
soups, 28, 39–42
soya bran, 34
spaghetti cheese in tomato sauce, 66
Spanish sauce, 122
spicy doughnuts, 107; *109*
sponge flan base, 83–4
steak and kidney pudding, 53
sugar, 25, 29
sulphapyridine, 20 ·
Swiss roll, 115

tartare sauce, 122
teabreads, 74–8
teenagers, gluten-free diet, 21–2
tomato: spaghetti cheese in tomato sauce, 66
tomato sauce, 121
tomato soup, 40
tuna: pasta salad, 43; *48*
salad Niçoise, 43

vegetable curry, 63
vegetable curry, 63–4
vegetarian dishes, 62–8
Victoria sandwich, 111–12; *110*

walnuts: chocolate nut fingers, 103–4
date and nut squares, 102–3
date and walnut loaf, 75–6; *70*
Welsh cheese cakes, 95
Welsh griddle cakes, 77–8; *79*
wheat: flour, 30
gluten content, 11
white bread, 71–2; *69*
white sauce, 120

yeast, 32, 68
Yorkshire pudding, 67